AFRICAN AMERICAN VOICES

AFRICAN AMERICAN VOICES

Volume 2: K-Z

Deborah Gillan Straub, *Editor*

®

AN IMPRINT OF GALE

AFRICAN AMERICAN VOICES

Deborah Gillan Straub, *Editor*

Staff

Sonia Benson, *U•X•L Developmental Editor*
Carol DeKane Nagel, *U•X•L Managing Editor*
Thomas L. Romig, *U•X•L Publisher*

Shanna Heilveil, *Production Associate*
Evi Seoud, *Assistant Production Manager*
Mary Beth Trimper, *Production Director*

Michelle DiMercurio, *Art Director*
Cynthia Baldwin, *Product Design Manager*

∞™ This book is printed on acid-free paper that meets the minimum requirements of American Nationa Standard for Information Sciences—Permanence Paper for Printed Library Materials, ANSI Z39.48 1984.

Library of Congress Catalog Card Number 96-060859
Printed in the United States of America

ISBN 0-8103-9497-9 (Set)
ISBN 0-8103-9498-7 (Volume 1)
ISBN 0-8103-9499-5 (Volume 2)

10 9 8 7 6 5 4 3 2

U•X•L is an imprint of Gale Research

Advisory Board

Contents

Frederick Douglass

Volume 1: A-J

Volume 2: K-Z

Speech Topics
at a Glance

Bold numerals indicate volume numbers.
For a more detailed listing of information
covered in these volumes, consult subject index.

Reader's Guide

Sojourner Truth

Orators have played key roles throughout the history of the United States, where the spoken word has helped shape foreign and domestic policy ever since the nation began over 200 years ago. *African American Voices* collects in a single source excerpted speeches delivered by African American civil rights activists, religious leaders, educators, feminists, abolitionists, politicians, writers, and other key figures who have changed the course of history by speaking out on a variety of issues.

Voices selections range from the well-known, such as Martin Luther King, Jr.'s "I Have a Dream" and Sojourner Truth's "Ain't I a Woman?" speeches, to lesser-known and harder-to-find entries, such as Fannie Lou Hamer's chilling testimony to the Democratic National Convention about her efforts to register to vote in Mississippi in 1962. Many of the speeches address various issues of civil rights and activism, but others delve into the arts, health, or personal adventures. Major movements and milestones of African American history are presented by speakers who were the central players in these events.

It is not possible in this first edition of *African American Voices* to include all of the many prominent African American speakers who have shaped American history. The thirty-six speechmakers featured in these volumes were chosen by a knowledgable team of advisors from a list of well over 100 candidates suitable to this collection. Due to the unavailability of certain materials for publication, some important speeches of the last two centuries were regretfully omitted from the set. Despite these omissions, however, *Voices* provides a compelling array of African American thought and issues from the past two centuries. Entries were selected: a) to encompass a wide range of perspectives and backgrounds; b) to be engaging and accessible to students; and c) to provide first-hand—and often quite dramatic—insight into the key issues, events, and movements of African American history.

The entries in *African American Voices* are arranged alphabetically by speaker. Each begins with introductory material, providing a brief biography of the speaker and the historical context of the speech that follows. Informative sidebars expand on topics mentioned within the entries. A "Sources" section, directing the student to further readings on the speechmaker and his or her speeches, concludes each entry.

African American Voices also contains more than 90 black-and-white illustrations, a subject index, a listing of speeches by major topics, and a timeline. Words and phrases are defined in the lower margin of the page on which they appear.

Related Reference Sources

African American Almanac features a comprehensive range of historical and current information on African American life and culture. Organized into twenty-six subject chapters, including civil rights, the family, the arts, religion, business and labor, politics, music, sports, and education, the volumes contain more than three hundred black-and-white photographs and maps, a selected bibliography, and a subject index.

African American Biography profiles three hundred African Americans, both living and deceased, prominent in fields ranging from civil rights to athletics, politics to literature, entertainment to science, religion to the military. A black-and-white portrait accompanies each entry, and an index lists all profilees by field of endeavor.

African American Chronology explores significant social, political, economic, cultural, and educational milestones in black history. The chronologically arranged volumes span from 1492 to modern times and contain more than one hundred illustrations, extensive cross references, and a subject index.

Acknowledgments

The editor wishes to thank the following people who served as advisors on this project: Wil A. Linkugel, Professor of Communication Studies, University of Kansas, Lawrence, Kansas; Jeanette J. Smith, Regional Coordinator, Julia Davis Branch, St. Louis Public Library, St. Louis, Missouri; and Hilda K. Weisburg, Media Specialist, Sayreville War Memorial High School, Parlin, New Jersey.

Your Suggestions Are Welcome

The editor welcomes your comments and suggestions for future editions of *African American Voices*. Please write: The Editor, *African American Voices*, U•X•L, 835 Penobscot Building, Detroit, Michigan 48226-4094; call toll-free: 1-800-877-4253; or fax: (313) 961-6348.

Introduction

Traditions in African American Oratory

Barbara Jordan

In the American tradition, there is a fundamental assumption that everyone has freedom of speech and the right to be heard in the public forum as guaranteed by the First Amendment to the Constitution. Imagine, then, the plight of some people in the United States who historically did not have freedom of speech—-African Americans. Because many of them were slaves from the seventeenth century until the Emancipation Proclamation freed them in 1863, they were not regarded as citizens. The U.S. Supreme Court reinforced this view in 1857 when it ruled that the Constitution had been written only for whites. Thus, as noncitizens without freedom of speech, blacks had to earn their "voice" in American society.

The roots of African American oratory can be traced back to oral African culture. In that environment, the human voice as well as drums were used to send messages, which another speaker or drummer would then respond to immediately. Both the original message and the answer were often quite creative and reflected the African religious belief in the spirit world.

Once in America, Africans continued their creative ways of communicating. During the time of slavery, these methods included field chants, hollers, and music, much of which had double or hidden meanings. This prevented the masters from knowing the true message, lest the slaves be punished for plotting against them.

Free blacks in the North, on the other hand, enjoyed freedom of speech to a degree their enslaved brothers in the South never could. Thus it was in the North that we heard speakers such as Frederick Douglass and Sojourner Truth. While some of these orators (such as Truth) could neither read nor write, they nevertheless spoke with passion and, more often than not, with strong religious conviction.

Given her reputation as an eloquent and persuasive speaker, Sojourner Truth is, in fact, a good example of what has made so many African American orators effective—-their delivery, their style, and their voice tones. Truth spoke in deep, sonorous tones and projected a sense of confidence. There was also a spiritual quality in her oratory that is common among many African American orators, including Martin Luther King, Jr., and Jesse Jackson. They all give the impression that God is on their side, a practice known as mythication.

While Sojourner Truth most notably reflects the spiritualist tradition in African American oratory, she was unique in other ways that have implications for how we understand African American oratory today. First, she was a woman; second, she was African American; third, she was illiterate; and fourth, she was poor. As a black woman who spoke before white audiences, she recognized the social distance between women and men and between African American women and white women. For her, race, gender, and class were barriers to be surmounted. Addressing these very same barriers in more recent times are African American women orators such as Fannie Lou Hamer and Shirley Chisholm.

While the written public record provides us with a fair amount of information about what the early black orators in the North had to say in their speeches, it is only in recent years that technology has allowed us to capture fully the interactive dynamics that typically occur between African American orators and their audiences. When both the speaker and his or her audience are black (and occasionally in racially-mixed groups as well), there is almost always a spontaneous verbal exchange that takes place known as call-response. This lively verbal interplay is unique to the African American oratorical tradition and has roots that extend back to Africa.

Many of the early black orators were preachers, and their congregations continued the African tradition of providing an immediate response to the message. These responses were both verbal and nonverbal, such as saying "Amen," "Hallelujah," or "Thank you, Lord," or waving one's hands or standing and pointing toward the preacher. In this way, the congregation affirmed the messenger and created collective harmony with him or her and with the Holy Spirit.

Nowadays, call-response is a way of uniting the orator and the audience so that they become substantially one, making the communication between them circular rather than one-way. The orator does not consider the verbal and nonverbal feedback from the audience as an interruption. In fact, many African American orators solicit this kind of feedback to determine whether they are reaching their audience, asking questions such as "Is anybody with me?" or "Can I get a witness?" The audience gives an immediate response ("Right on," "Make it plain," "Go 'head," "Take your time"), and this in turn affirms the messenger and urges him or her on to greater oratorical heights.

In addition to documenting this colorful tradition, modern technology has also helped preserve the accuracy of black oratory. Accuracy is always a concern when orators speak without a written text or when the written text is not saved. For example, since Sojourner Truth did not write down her speeches, there is now some question as to the accuracy of the existing printed texts.

The importance of technology in establishing accuracy is also evident when oratory contains a combination of prepared written text and extemporaneous speech, as in Martin Luther King, Jr.'s "I Have a Dream" speech. Audio and video recordings allow us to pinpoint when King dispensed with the text and began to speak extemporaneously. Such recordings also play a vital role in helping us to hear the moving musical qualities of his voice.

While Sojourner Truth and Martin Luther King, Jr., represent the extremes of literacy in African American oratory, each was effective due to their mastery of language and their ethos. Like most African American orators, they felt an urgency to give voice to the needs of their people. Both spoke and gained recognition through the courage of their convictions.

Dorthy L. Pennington
Associate Professor
University of Kansas
Lawrence, Kansas

Suggested Readings

Boulware, Marcus H., *The Oratory of Negro Leaders, 1900— 1968,* Negro Universities Press, 1969.

Foner, Philip S., editor, *The Voice of Black America: Major Speeches by Negroes in the United States, 1797–1971,* Simon & Schuster, 1972.

Gonzalez, Alberto, Marsha Houston, and Victoria Chen, editors, *Our Voices: Essays in Culture, Ethnicity and Communication,* Roxbury Publishing Company, 1994.

Halliburton, Warren J., *Historic Speeches of African Americans,* F. Watts, 1993.

Credits

Grateful acknowledgment is made to the following sources whose works appear in this volume. Every effort has been made to trace copyright, but if omissions have been made, please contact the publisher.

Carmichael, Stokely. From "Berkeley Speech" in *Stokely Speaks: Black Power Back to Pan-Africanism.* Random House, 1971. Reprinted by permission of the author.

Carson, Ben. From a speech delivered on June 27, 1994, at the Million Dollar Roundtable Convention in Dallas, Texas. Reprinted by permission of the author.

Cleaver, Eldridge. *The Black Panther,* v. 2, March 16, 1968, for "Political Struggle in America," by Eldridge Cleaver. Reprinted by permission of the author.

Dove, Rita. From a speech, "Who's Afraid of Poetry?," delivered on March 17, 1994, at the National Press Club. Reprinted by permission of the author.

Edelman, Marian Wright. From a speech delivered on June 9, 1994, at the Harvard University Medical School in Cambridge, Massachusetts. Reprinted by permission of the author. Marian Wright Edelman is the founder and president of the Children's Defense Fund.

ed Methodist National Youth Ministry Organization, conference on youth and violence. Copyright © 1993 by the General Board of Church and Society of The United Methodist Church. Reprinted by permission of the publisher.

Young, Whitney M., Jr. *Vital Speeches of the Day,* v. XXXVI, September 15, 1970. Reprinted by permission of the publisher.

The photographs and illustrations appearing in African American Voices were received from the following sources:

Cover: Malcolm X. UPI/Corbis-Bettmann.

Timeline: Courtesy of the Library of Congress: xxvii (top), xxviii (bottom), xxix (bottom); **The Bettmann Archive/ Newsphotos, Inc.:** xxix (top), xxxi, xxxii (top), xxxii (bottom), xxxiii (bottom), xxxiv (top), xxxvi; **U.S. Army Photograph:** xxx; **AP/Wide World Photos:** xxxiii (top), xxxv.

The Bettmann Archive/Newsphotos, Inc.: pp. 6, 57, 78, 101, 139, 188, 207, 226, 235, 247, 349, 405; **AP/Wide World Photos:** pp. 8, 21, 35, 39, 46, 57, 59, 64, 69, 113, 119, 136, 147, 165, 195, 203, 215, 254, 259, 268, 275, 281, 287, 316, 321, 323; **U.S. Senate Historical Office:** p. 11; **Archive Photos, Inc.:** pp. 31, 231, 333, 359,: **Library of Congress:** pp. 17, 73, 81, 83, 103, 129, 241, 245, 303, 353, 356, 368, 376; **Chris Felver:** p. 87; **Children's Television Workshop:** p. 95; **The Granger Collection Ltd.:** pp. 119, 125, 309; **Lou Jones Studio:** p. 291; **University of Chicago Library:** p. 363; **U.S. Signal Corps. of National Archives:** p. 383; **National Urban League:** p. 399.

Timeline of Important African American Events

1776–1996

Boldface indicates speakers featured in these volumes

American Revolution to the Antislavery Movement, 1776–1860

1787 The Continental Congress bans slavery in the Northwest Territory.

1790 The first U.S. Naturalization Act allows only "free white persons" to become American citizens.

1791 The Bill of Rights (the first ten amendments to the Constitution) is ratified.

1793 Congress passes the first Fugitive Slave Law, making it a crime to hide an escaped slave.

1831 Nat Turner leads the most famous slave rebellion in American history. He is quickly captured and hanged.

1832 **Maria W. Miller Stewart** becomes the first American-born woman to give a public speech.

1843 At a national convention of black men held in Buffalo, New York, **Henry Highland Garnet** delivers a fiery speech urging slaves to revolt.

Nat Turner's capture

1776	1787	1812–1815	1848
Declaration of Independence	U.S. Constitution approved	War of 1812	Seneca Falls Convention for women's rights

• • **1760** • • **1780** • • **1800** • • **1820** • • **1840** • •

Civil War poster urging blacks to join Union Army

1850 Congress approves the Compromise of 1850, which outlaws slave trade in Washington, D.C., allows it to continue throughout the South, and admits California to the Union as a free state.

1851 At a women's rights convention in Ohio, **Sojourner Truth** delivers her famous "Ain't I a Woman?" speech.

1852 **Frederick Douglass** delivers his powerful "Fourth of July Oration."

1857 The Supreme Court issues its *Dred Scott* decision, ruling that blacks cannot become citizens and have no rights under the Constitution, and that Congress has no power to prohibit slavery in any part of U.S. territory.

1859 White abolitionist John Brown raids the federal arsenal at Harpers Ferry, Virginia, to obtain weapons for slaves to use in a revolt against their masters. He is captured and executed.

Civil War and Reconstruction, 1861–1880

1862 Congress authorizes President Abraham Lincoln to accept blacks for service in the Union Army.

1863 President Lincoln issues the Emancipation Proclamation, freeing slaves in the states then at war against the Union.

1865 President Andrew Johnson announces his Reconstruction program for reorganizing and rebuilding the southern states.

Congress ratifies the 13th Amendment, which outlaws slavery in the United States.

1868 Congress ratifies the 14th Amendment, which recognizes blacks as American citizens with certain constitutional guarantees.

Abraham Lincoln at the first reading of the Emancipation Proclamation

1860
South Carolina secedes from the Union

1861
Confederate States of America form; Civil War begins

1865
Civil War ends; Reconstruction Era begins in South

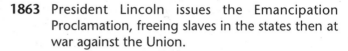

• • **1850** • • **1855** • • **1860** • • **1865** • • **1868** • •

1870 Congress ratifies the 15th Amendment, which states that no male American citizen can be denied the right to vote.

1875 Congress passes a civil rights bill (known as the Civil Rights Act of 1875) that outlaws discrimination in public places and on public transportation.

Blanche Kelso Bruce becomes the only black man to serve a full term in the Senate until the mid-twentieth century.

Booker T. Washington

Pioneers in Civil Rights, 1881–1926

1881 Booker T. Washington opens the Tuskegee Institute in Alabama.

1883 The Supreme Court overturns the Civil Rights Act of 1875.

1892 **Ida B. Wells-Barnett** launches an anti-lynching campaign with a series of newspaper editorials that angrily expose the truth behind many of the attacks.

1895 **Booker T. Washington** delivers his "Atlanta Compromise" address.

1896 The Supreme Court issues its *Plessy v. Ferguson* decision upholding the "separate but equal" doctrine regarding the use of public places and public transportation by blacks.

1901 U.S. Representative **George H. White** of North Carolina delivers an impassioned farewell address to his colleagues upon leaving the House after two terms. More than twenty years pass before any other African Americans are elected to Congress.

1903 An essay in **W. E. B. Du Bois**'s book *The Souls of Black Folk* criticizes **Booker T. Washington,** touching off a bitter feud between the two leaders.

W. E. B. Du Bois

1870 Women organize nationally to obtain vote	1877 Reconstruction Era ends	1886 Samuel Gompers forms the American Federation of Labor	1898 Spanish-American War

Soldiers in World War II: 92nd (Negro) Division, Italy, 1944

1905 The Niagara Movement, the forerunner of the National Association for the Advancement of Colored People (NAACP), takes shape at a meeting in New York State. Many prominent black leaders attend, including **W. E. B. Du Bois** and **Ida B. Wells-Barnett**.

1909 The National Association for the Advancement of Colored People is founded. **W. E. B. Du Bois** serves as editor of its official publication, the *Crisis*.

1910 The National Urban League is founded.

1915 **Booker T. Washington** dies.

1916 **Marcus Garvey** establishes a branch of his Universal Negro Improvement Association in New York City.

1919 Led by **W. E. B. Du Bois,** the first Pan-African Congress meets in Paris, France.

Fighting Segregation, 1926–1960

1936 President Franklin D. Roosevelt appoints **Mary McLeod Bethune** to his unofficial "Black Cabinet." Among the president's other African American advisors is **Ralph Bunche**.

1941 President Roosevelt issues an executive order banning racial discrimination in the defense industry and in government training programs.

1944 **Adam Clayton Powell, Jr.,** is elected to the U.S. House of Representatives from a newly created district that includes the Harlem neighborhood of New York City, making him the first black congressman from the East.

1908
Henry Ford
unveils Model T

1914–1918
World War I

1929
Stock market crashes;
Great Depression
begins

1939–1945
World War II

1948 President Harry S Truman issues an executive order calling for equality of treatment and opportunity for all Americans in the armed forces, thus officially ending segregation and discrimination in the military.

1950 **Ralph Bunche** becomes the first black to win the Nobel Peace Prize.

1952 **Malcolm X** is paroled from prison and soon becomes a minister in the Nation of Islam.

1954 The Supreme Court issues its landmark *Brown v. Board of Education of Topeka* decision overturning *Plessy v. Ferguson* and declaring racial segregation in public schools unconstitutional. Attorney **Thurgood Marshall** leads the NAACP legal team that argues the case before the justices.

Thurgood Marshall standing in front of Supreme Court, 1958

1955 **Roy Wilkins** becomes executive secretary of the NAACP.

Martin Luther King, Jr., launches a year-long bus boycott in Montgomery, Alabama, after Rosa Parks is arrested for refusing to give up her seat on a city bus to a white person.

1957 The Southern Christian Leadership Conference (SCLC) is cofounded by **Martin Luther King, Jr.;** he serves as its first president.

Federal troops are sent to Little Rock, Arkansas, to stop local residents from interfering with the desegregation of a local public high school.

Congress passes the Voting Rights Bill of 1957, the first major civil rights legislation since 1875.

1959 **Lorraine Hansberry**'s play *A Raisin in the Sun* becomes the first play by a black woman to open on Broadway.

1945	**1950**		**1959**
Cold War begins between U.S. and Soviet Union	Senator Joseph McCarthy begins crusade against communists	**1950–1953** Korean War	Fidel Castro leads successful revolution in Cuba

• • 1947 • • 1950 • • 1953 • • 1956 • • 1959 • •

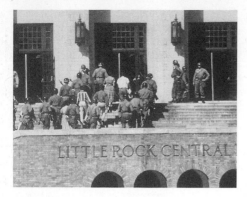

Federal troops escort black students during desegregation at Little Rock, Arkansas, High School

Civil Rights Activism, 1960–1965

1960 The Student Nonviolent Coordinating Committee (SNCC) is founded in the wake of civil rights sit-ins and demonstrations by young people throughout much of the South.

1961 **Whitney M. Young, Jr.,** becomes executive director of the National Urban League.

1963 **Martin Luther King, Jr.,** delivers his "I Have a Dream" speech to a crowd of more than 200,000 assembled at the Lincoln Memorial for the massive March on Washington civil rights demonstration.

1964 Congress ratifies the 24th Amendment, which outlaws the use of the poll tax to prevent people from voting.

Malcolm X drops out of the Nation of Islam to start his own movement.

Congress passes the Civil Rights Act of 1964, which prohibits discrimination in hiring and employment practices and paves the way for various affirmative action programs.

Martin Luther King, Jr., receives the Nobel Peace Prize.

Fannie Lou Hamer cofounds the Mississippi Freedom Democratic Party.

1965 **Malcolm X** is assassinated.

Led by **Martin Luther King, Jr.,** the SCLC launches a voter registration drive in Selma, Alabama, that escalates into a nationwide protest movement and ends in the famous "Freedom March" from Selma to Montgomery.

Martin Luther King, Jr., leads march from Selma to Montgomery, Alabama, 1965

1960
Militant student
movement begins
to organize

1963
President
John F. Kennedy
is assassinated

1965
United State sends
combat troops
to Vietnam

1965 Congress passes the Voting Rights Act of 1965, which prevents states from denying the right to vote to people unable or unwilling to pay a poll tax and to those unable to read or write English.

Racial disturbances erupt in the Watts ghetto of Los Angeles, California.

Burning buildings, Detroit riots, 1967

Black Power, 1966–1973

1966 **Stokely Carmichael** becomes head of the Student Nonviolent Coordinating Committee and promotes the concept of "black power."

Huey Newton and Bobby Seale establish the Black Panther Party. **Eldridge Cleaver** joins them and becomes a key spokesperson for the group.

1967 Race riots occur in Newark, New Jersey, Detroit, Michigan, and several other U.S. cities.

The Supreme Court rules unconstitutional all laws prohibiting interracial marriage.

Thurgood Marshall is sworn in as the first black justice of the Supreme Court.

1968 **Martin Luther King, Jr.**, is assassinated.

The new head of the SCLC, Ralph Abernathy, leads a group of blacks, whites, Native Americans, and Mexican Americans on a march to Washington, D.C., known as the "Poor People's Campaign."

The Kerner Commission releases the results of its investigation into the causes of the 1967 race riots, concluding that "white racism" was largely to blame.

Shirley Chisholm wins a seat in the House of Representatives, becoming the first black woman ever to serve in Congress.

Shirley Chisholm, 1972

1965	1966	1968
Demonstrators protest U.S. involvement in Vietnam War	National Organization for Women (NOW) is founded	Student protest demonstrations hit 221 U.S. campuses

• • **1965** • • **1966** • • **1967** • • **1968** • •

Jesse Jackson giving thumbs up to announce his candidacy for president, 1987

1969 The Supreme Court rules that public school districts must end racial segregation immediately.

1970 Racial violence erupts in school districts across the United States as court-ordered desegregation plans are implemented that continue through 1976.

1970 The Voting Rights Act of 1965 is extended until 1975.

1971 The Supreme Court rules that busing students to achieve racial desegregation is constitutional.

1972 **Shirley Chisholm** becomes the first black and the first woman to seek the Democratic nomination for president.

1973 **Marion Wright Edelman** establishes the Children's Defense Fund.

Milestones, 1974–1990

1974 After a series of hearings, the House Judiciary Committee—including **Barbara Jordan** of Texas—adopts three articles of impeachment against President Richard M. Nixon.

1975 The Voting Rights Act of 1965 is extended for an additional seven years.

1976 The Supreme Court rules that blacks and other minorities are entitled to retroactive job security.

Representative Barbara Jordan delivers a rousing keynote address at the Democratic National Convention.

1977 **Alex Haley** is awarded a special Pulitzer Prize for *Roots*.

1978 The Supreme Court issues its *Bakke* decision, declaring racial and ethnic quota systems in college admissions unconstitutional.

Bakke decision protest march

1969	1973	1974	1979–1981
U.S. astronaut Neil Armstrong walks on moon	United States signs cease-fire with North Vietnam	President Richard M. Nixon resigns after Watergate investigation	Fifty-two hostages are held at U.S. Embassy in Iran

1980   Miami, Florida, is the scene of the most serious racial disturbances in the country since the riots of the 1960s.

1986   The first national **Martin Luther King, Jr.,** holiday is celebrated.

Dr. **Ben Carson** performs the first successful separation of Siamese twins joined at the back of the head.

1988   Jesse Jackson places second behind Michael Dukakis in the delegate count to win the Democratic party's nomination for president of the United States.

1989   General **Colin Powell** becomes the first black chairman of the Joint Chiefs of Staff.

Clarence Thomas

The 1990s

1991   In Los Angeles, California, the beating of black motorist Rodney King by four white policemen is captured on videotape and broadcast on network news programs, sparking an international outcry.

Thurgood Marshall retires from the Supreme Court.

Clarence Thomas is confirmed for the Supreme Court after controversial hearings during which University of Oklahoma law professor Anita Hill accuses him of sexual harassment.

1992   Racial violence erupts in Los Angeles, California, after four white police officers are acquitted in the beating of black motorist Rodney King.

Carol Moseley-Braun of Illinois becomes the first black woman elected to the U.S. Senate.

1993   **Rita Dove** is named poet laureate of the United States.

Toni Morrison becomes the first black woman to win the Nobel Prize for literature.

1981
Sandra Day O'Connor becomes the first woman member of the Supreme Court

1989
German reunification; Berlin Wall falls

1990–1991
Persian Gulf War

1991
Dissolution of the Soviet Union; Cold War ends

• • **1980** • • **1983** • • **1985** • • **1988** • • **1990** • • **1993** • •

The Million Man March, Washington, D.C., 1995

1994 In the mid-term elections, the Republicans regain majorities in both the House of Representatives and the Senate for the first time in forty years.

1995 Republicans in Congress begin work on the reforms and budget cuts proposed in their "Contract with America." Opponents such as Jesse Jackson and **Marian Wright Edelman** condemn the "Contract" as devastating to the poor, children, and the elderly.

In two separate decisions written by Justice **Clarence Thomas,** the Supreme Court comes out in favor of sharply limiting federal affirmative-action programs and court-ordered school integration efforts.

The Supreme Court declares unconstitutional the practice of using race as the major factor in drawing legislative districts.

Led by Nation of Islam leader Louis Farrakhan and former NAACP executive director Benjamin Chavis, the "Million Man March" attracts hundreds of thousands of African American men to Washington, D.C., to promote black self-help and self-discipline.

Retired General **Colin Powell** announces that he will not run for president in 1996.

1996 The Children's Defense Fund and **Marian Wright Edelman** organize a "Stand for Children" march and rally on June 1 in Washington, D.C.

1994
North American Free
Trade Agreement
(NAFTA) goes into effect

1995
Bombing of Federal
Building in Tulsa,
Oklahoma

1996
Israeli Prime Minister
Yitzhak Rabin is
assassinated

AFRICAN AMERICAN VOICES

Martin Luther King, Jr.

1929–1968

Civil rights activist

Martin Luther King, Jr., is considered one of the outstanding orators (public speakers) of the twentieth century. He used his skills as a communicator to become the intellectual and spiritual guiding force of the civil rights movement during the years of its greatest triumphs. His words—both written and spoken—powerfully brought his cause to America's social, political, and religious awareness. By combining his Christian-influenced ideals with the techniques of nonviolence as practiced by India's Mohandas Gandhi, he gave the civil rights struggle a new sense of urgency and high moral purpose.

Early Life

King was born in Atlanta, Georgia. He was the son of Martin Luther King, Sr., a prominent black minister, and Alberta Williams King, a teacher. After attending local primary and secondary schools, young Martin continued his education in his hometown at Morehouse College. At first, he felt

"IT WOULD BE FATAL FOR THE NATION TO OVERLOOK THE URGENCY OF THE MOVEMENT AND TO UNDERESTIMATE THE DETERMINATION OF THE NEGRO. THIS SWELTERING SUMMER OF THE NEGRO'S LEGITIMATE DISCONTENT WILL NOT PASS UNTIL THERE IS AN INVIGORATING AUTUMN OF FREEDOM AND EQUALITY. NINETEEN-SIXTY-THREE IS NOT AN END BUT A BEGINNING."

no particular calling to the religious life. But with the encouragement and support of Morehouse's president, Dr. Benjamin Mays, King came to realize that he could achieve personal and professional fulfillment as a minister. Therefore,
after earning his bachelor's degree, he went on to attend
Crozer Theological Seminary and then Boston University.

By the time King received his doctorate degree from
Boston University in 1955, he was already pastor of the
Dexter Avenue Baptist Church in Montgomery, Alabama.
There, in 1955, he first captured national attention as one
of the leaders of the black community's famous city-wide
bus boycott after Rosa Parks, a highly-respected local
seamstress, was hauled off to jail for violating segregation
laws on a city bus. It was, in fact, in connection with this
boycott that King made what qualifies as his first public
speech on civil rights. Upon hearing of Parks' arrest, local
black leaders called a meeting to map out a plan of action.
Turning to the new, young minister in town—he was just
twenty-six years old—they asked him to deliver the main
address of the evening.

In 1957, two years after the bus boycott, King cofounded the Southern Christian Leadership Conference (SCLC),
and was chosen as the group's first president. The SCLC's
chief goal was to obtain equal rights for blacks through
aggressive but nonviolent action such as protest marches
and voter-registration drives.

In 1960, King and his family moved back to Atlanta,
where he became co-pastor (with his father) of Ebenezer
Baptist Church. It was not long, however, before he had
given up his responsibilities as a minister to devote all of his
time to the SCLC and its fight for justice. Time and time
again, King braved hostile crowds and the possibility of
arrest and jail to focus attention on the immorality of racial
discrimination. He also worked to give blacks a more positive self-image and sense of direction.

Throughout that year, for example, King lent his support
to the student sit-in movement then expanding rapidly
across the South. Speaking to demonstrators, he encouraged them to continue resisting segregation with nonvio-

The Student Sit-In Movement

In 1960 the "sit-in," a form of nonviolent protest against segregation, began in North Carolina and quickly swept across the South. Led mostly by black college students, the first sit-ins took place at lunch counters that denied service to black customers. Demonstrators typically sat down at the counter (or on the floor nearby) and quietly but firmly refused to move to make room for white customers. Despite being punched, kicked, beaten, and hauled off to jail, the students would not fight back or leave the premises. This protest strategy, known as passive resistance, proved to be so successful that up-and-coming civil rights activists such as Martin Luther King, Jr., soon adopted it for use against other forms of discrimination.

The sit-in movement also led to the founding of the Student Nonviolent Coordinating Committee (SNCC, or "Snick"), one of the best-known civil rights groups of the 1960s. The SNCC attracted many black and white college students who helped organize protests and register black voters. **Stokely Carmichael** (see entry) served briefly as head of SNCC around 1966 before joining the more radical Black Panther Party.

lent action. He also took part in many sit-ins himself and was arrested for his activities.

In April 1963, King launched a series of large-scale anti-discrimination protests in Birmingham, Alabama. He and his fellow civil rights activists were met with force by the city's police, who used dogs and high-powered water hoses to break up the crowds. Scenes of demonstrators being brutalized and arrested appeared on evening news programs and in newspapers and magazines and did much to sway public opinion against Birmingham city officials, especially in the North. Finally, the two sides reached an agreement on May 10 calling for the gradual desegregation of public accommodations.

King made use of every opportunity to take his message to America and the world through his writings and speeches. It was a message he always delivered with emotion and drama, relying on words and rhythms shaped by his southern background and religious training to touch and inspire his listeners.

Probably the most stirring and memorable example of his many public speeches is the one he gave in Washing-

ton, D.C., on August 28, 1963. About 250,000 people had gathered in front of the Lincoln Memorial to demand that Congress pass sweeping civil rights legislation. Facing that massive crowd as well as a national television audience and members of the press from all over the world, King delivered his strikingly intense and dramatic "I Have a Dream" speech. His remarks affirmed that the civil rights struggle was a moral crusade of the highest order. The speech is reprinted here from Roy L. Hill's book Rhetoric of Racial Revolt, *Golden Bell Press, 1964.*

❝

I am happy to join with you today in what will go down in history as the greatest demonstration for freedom in the history of our nation.

Five **score** years ago, a great American, in whose symbolic shadow we stand today, signed the Emancipation Proclamation. This momentous **decree** came as a great beacon of light of hope to millions of Negro slaves who had been seared in the flames of withering injustice. It came as a joyous daybreak to end the long night of their captivity.

But one hundred years later, the Negro still is not free. One hundred years later, the life of the Negro is still sadly crippled by the **manacles** of segregation and the chains of discrimination.

One hundred years later, the Negro lives on a lonely island of poverty in the midst of a vast ocean of material prosperity. One hundred years later, the Negro is still **languished** in the corners of American society and finds himself an **exile** in his own land. So we have come here today to dramatize a shameful condition.

In a sense we have come to our nation's capital to cash a check. When the architects of our republic wrote the magnificent words of the Constitution and the Declaration of Independence, they were signing a **promissory note** to which every American was to **fall heir.** This note was a promise that all men, yes, black men as well as white men, would be granted the **unalienable** rights of life, liberty, and the pursuit of happiness.

score: twenty.

decree: an order, usually with the force of law.

manacles: handcuffs; restraints.

languished: in a state of weakness or neglect.

exile: a person forced to leave his or her home or country.

promissory note: a written promise to pay a person or group at a future date.

fall heir: eventually inherit.

unalienable: incapable of being withdrawn or given up.

Martin Luther King, Jr.

It is obvious today that America has **defaulted** on this promissory note insofar as her citizens of color are concerned. Instead of honoring this sacred obligation, America has given the Negro people a bad check; which has come back marked "insufficient funds."

But we refuse to believe that the bank of justice is bankrupt. We refuse to believe that there are insufficient funds in the great vaults of opportunity of this nation. So we have come to cash this check—a check that will give us upon demand the riches of freedom and the security of justice.

We have also come to this **hallowed** spot to remind America of the fierce urgency of now. This is no time to engage in the luxury of cooling off or to take the tranquilizing drug of gradualism. Now is the time to make real the promises of democracy. Now is the time to rise from the dark and desolate valley of segregation to the sunlit path of racial justice. Now is time to lift our nation from the quicksands of racial injustice to the solid rock of brotherhood. Now is the time to make justice a reality for all of God's children.

King delivering his "I Have a Dream" speech

It would be fatal for the nation to overlook the urgency of the movement and to underestimate the determination of the Negro. This sweltering summer of the Negro's legitimate discontent will not pass until there is an **invigorating** autumn of freedom and equality. Nineteen-sixty-three is not an end but a beginning. Those who hope that the Negro needed to blow off steam and will now be content will have a rude awakening if the nation returns to business as usual.

There will be neither rest nor **tranquility** in America until the Negro is granted his citizenship rights. The whirl-winds of revolt will continue to shake the foundations of our nation until the bright day of justice emerges.

But there is something that I must say to my people who stand on the warm threshold which leads into the palace of

defaulted: failed to meet an obligation.

hallowed: sacred, holy.

invigorating: lively, energetic.

tranquility: peace, quiet.

justice. In the process of gaining our rightful place we must not be guilty of wrongful deeds.

Let us not seek to satisfy our thirst for freedom by drinking from the cup of bitterness and hatred. We must forever conduct our struggle on the high plane of dignity and discipline. We must not allow our creative protest to degenerate into physical violence. Again and again we must rise to the majestic heights of meeting physical force with soul force.

The marvelous new militancy which has engulfed the Negro community must not lead us to a distrust of all white people, for many of our white brothers, as evidenced by their presence here today, have come to realize that their destiny is tied up with our destiny and they have come to realize that their freedom is **inextricably** bound to our freedom. This offense we share mounted to storm the battlements of injustice must be carried forth by a biracial army. We cannot walk alone.

And as we walk, we must make the pledge that we shall always march ahead. We cannot turn back. There are those who are asking the **devotees** of civil rights, "When will you be satisfied?" We can never be satisfied as long as the Negro is the victim of the unspeakable horrors of police brutality.

We can never be satisfied as long as our bodies, heavy with the fatigue of travel, cannot gain lodging in the motels of the highways and the hotels of the cities. We cannot be satisfied as long as the Negro's basic mobility is from a smaller ghetto to a larger one.

We can never be satisfied as long as our children are stripped of their selfhood and robbed of their dignity by signs stating "for whites only." We cannot be satisfied as long as a Negro in Mississippi cannot vote and a Negro in New York believes he has nothing for which to vote. No, we are not satisfied, and we will not be satisfied until justice rolls down like waters and righteousness like a mighty stream.

I am not **unmindful** that some of you have come here out of excessive trials and tribulation. Some of you have come fresh from narrow jail cells. Some of you have come from areas where your quest for freedom left you battered by the storms of persecution and staggered by the winds of

inextricably: incapable of being untied or untangled.

devotees: supporters.

unmindful: unaware.

Martin Luther King, Jr.

police brutality.... Continue to work with the faith that unearned suffering is **redemptive.**

Go back to Mississippi; go back to Alabama; go back to South Carolina; go back to Georgia; go back to Louisiana; go back to the slums and ghettos of the Northern cities, knowing that somehow this situation can, and will be changed. Let us not **wallow** in the valley of despair.

So I say to you, my friends, that even though we must face the difficulties of today and tomorrow, I still have a dream. It is a dream deeply rooted in the American dream that one day this nation will rise up and live out the true meaning of its **creed**—we hold these truths to be self evident, that all men are created equal.

I have a dream that one day on the red hills of Georgia, sons of former slaves and sons of former slaveowners will be able to sit down together at the table of brotherhood.

I have a dream that one day, even the state of Mississippi, a state sweltering with the heat of injustice, sweltering with the heat of oppression, will be transformed into an oasis of freedom and justice.

I have a dream my four little children will one day live in a nation where they will not be judged by the color of their skin but by content of their character. I have a dream today!

I have a dream that one day, down in Alabama, with its vicious racists..., that one day, right there in Alabama, little black boys and black girls will be able to join hands with little white boys and white girls as sisters and brothers. I have a dream today!

I have a dream that one day every valley shall be exalted, every hill and mountain shall be made low, the rough places shall be made plain, and the crooked places shall be made straight and the glory of the Lord will be revealed and all flesh shall see it together.

This is our hope. This is the faith that I go back to the South with.

With this faith we will be able to hear out of the mountain of despair a stone of hope. With this faith we will be able to transform the jangling **discords** of our nation into a beautiful symphony of brotherhood.

redemptive: capable of reforming something or making it more worthwhile.

wallow: roll around in; excessively indulge in.

creed: belief.

discords: lack of agreement or harmony.

With this faith we will be able to work together to pray together, to struggle together, to go to jail together, to stand up for freedom together, knowing that we will be free one day. This will be the day when all of God's children will be able to sing with new meaning—"my country 'tis of thee; sweet land of liberty; of thee I sing; land where my fathers died, land of the pilgrim's pride; from every mountain side, let freedom ring"—and if America is to be a great nation, this must become true.

So let freedom ring from the **prodigious** hilltops of New Hampshire.

Let freedom ring from the mighty mountains of New York.

Let freedom ring from the heightening Alleghenies of Pennsylvania.

Let freedom ring from the snow-capped Rockies of Colorado.

Let freedom ring from the curvaceous slopes of California.

But not only that.

Let freedom ring from Stone Mountain of Georgia.

Let freedom ring from Lookout Mountain of Tennessee.

Let freedom ring from every hill and molehill of Mississippi, from every mountainside, let freedom ring.

And when we allow freedom to ring, when we let it ring from every village and hamlet, from every state and city, we will be able to speed up that day when all of God's children— black men and white men, Jews and Gentiles, Catholics and Protestants—will be able to join hands and to sing in the words of the old Negro spiritual, "Free at last, free at last; thank God Almighty, we are free at last."

99

On December 10, 1964, King became the youngest person and only the second African American to win the Nobel Peace Prize. It was presented to him in honor of his commitment to nonviolent resistance to racial oppression. Just a few weeks later, King launched a massive voter registration drive in Selma, Alabama. Over the next three months, the

prodigious: impressively large; extraordinary, amazing.

Martin Luther King, Jr.

situation grew very tense between civil rights activists and the angry whites who opposed them. Before long, the protest had attracted nationwide attention. King and his supporters had to endure brutal violence—some of it at the hands of Alabama state troopers—and many of them (including King) were arrested.

Beginning March 21, 1965, thousands of demonstrators staged a fifty-mile-long "Freedom March" from Selma to the city of Montgomery to dramatize their struggle. On March 25, about fifty thousand people gathered in front of the state capitol building to listen to their leaders criticize Alabama officials for interfering with their voting rights. King, of course, was one of those speakers. His address brought the protest to an end with the triumphant image

King and his wife, Coretta Scott King, lead civil rights march from Selma to Montgomery, Alabama, 1965

of a march toward justice that nothing and no one had the power to stop.

King's work in the South gradually chipped away at some of the foundations of racial discrimination there. He met with less success working in the North, however. In mid-1966, for example, an attempt to rally blacks in Chicago to challenge Mayor Richard Daley and his policy of segregation fell far short of King's goals. By 1967, it was clear to him and others in the mainstream civil rights movement that their message of Christian brotherhood and peaceful protest had little appeal to young, angry blacks in the urban ghettos of the North.

*By this time, too, the Vietnam War was beginning to claim more and more of the money and attention once devoted to the fight against poverty and racial injustice. Although he had often expressed his belief in world peace, King had been reluctant to reveal his strong personal opposition to the Vietnam War. He was afraid that admitting he was against the war might **antagonize** too many of his supporters. But in early 1967, King linked himself publicly with the antiwar movement hoping to form a new coalition of people who were committed to both peace in Vietnam and civil rights for blacks.*

*In April 1968, King was in Memphis, Tennessee. He had gone there to show his support for striking city sanitation workers and to help in the effort to organize them into a labor union. There, on the evening of April 3, King delivered what turned out to be his last speech. In it, he referred to having seen the promised land but expressed doubts that he would actually get to visit. His words proved to be mysteriously and somewhat frighteningly **prophetic**. The excerpt here is reprinted from James Melvin Washington's A Testament of Hope: The Essential Writings of Martin Luther King, Jr., Harper & Row, 1986.*

" "

If I were standing at the beginning of time..., and the Almighty said to me, "Martin Luther King, which age would you like to live in?"—I would take my mental flight by

antagonize: provoke, annoy.

prophetic: capable of predicting the future.

Martin Luther King, Jr.

Egypt through, or rather across the Red Sea, through the wilderness on toward the promised land. And in spite of its magnificence, I wouldn't stop there. I would move on by Greece, and take my mind to Mount Olympus. And I would see [the philosophers] Plato, Aristotle, Socrates, Euripides and Aristophanes assembled around the **Parthenon** as they discussed the great and eternal issues of reality.

But I wouldn't stop there. I would go on, even to the great **heyday** of the Roman Empire. And I would see developments around there, through various emperors and leaders. But I wouldn't stop there. I would even come up to the day of the Renaissance, and get a quick picture of all that the Renaissance did for the cultural and **esthetic** life of man. But I wouldn't stop there. I would even go by the way that the man for whom I'm named had his **habitat.** And I would watch Martin Luther as he tacked his ninety-five theses on the door at the church in Wittenberg. [King is referring here to German religious leader Martin Luther. During the 1500s, his objections to certain practices of the Roman Catholic Church started what is known as the Reformation. This in turn led to the founding of the various Protestant churches.]

But I wouldn't stop there. I would come on up even to 1863, and watch a **vacillating** president by the name of Abraham Lincoln finally come to the conclusion that he had to sign the Emancipation Proclamation. But I wouldn't stop there. I would even come up to the early thirties, and see a man [President Franklin Roosevelt] **grappling** with the problems of the bankruptcy of his nation....

But I wouldn't stop there. Strangely enough, I would turn to the Almighty, and say, "If you allow me to live just a few years in the second half of the twentieth century, I will be happy." Now that's a strange statement. But I know, somehow, that only when it is dark enough, can you see the stars. And I see God working in this period of the twentieth century in a way that men, in some strange way, are responding—something is happening in our world. The masses of people are rising up. And wherever they are assembled today ... the cry is always the same—"We want to be free."

And another reason that I'm happy to live in this period is that we have been forced to a point where we're going to

Parthenon: an ancient temple that stands on a hill in the city of Athens, Greece.

heyday: the time in life when a person or a group was strongest and most active.

esthetic: artistic.

habitat: home.

vacillating: hesitant, wavering.

grappling: wrestling, struggling.

have to grapple with the problems that men have been trying to grapple with through history.... Survival demands that we grapple with them. Men, for years now, have been talking about war and peace. But now, no longer can they just talk about it. It is no longer a choice between violence and nonviolence in this world; it's nonviolence or nonexistence.

That is where we are today. And also in the human rights revolution, if something isn't done, and in a hurry, to bring the colored peoples of the world out of their long years of poverty, their long years of hurt and neglect, the whole world is doomed. Now, I'm just happy that God has allowed me to live in this period, to see what is unfolding....

I can remember ... when Negroes were just going around ... scratching where they didn't itch, and laughing when they were not tickled. But that day is all over. We mean business now, and we are determined to gain our rightful place in God's world.

And that's all this whole thing is about. We aren't engaged in any negative protest and in any negative arguments with anybody. We are saying that we are determined to be men. We are determined to be people. We are saying that we are God's children. And that we don't have to live like we are forced to live.

Now, what does all of this mean in this great period of history? It means that we've got to stay together. We've got to stay together and maintain unity....

Secondly, let us keep the issues where they are. The issue is injustice. The issue is the refusal of Memphis to be fair and honest in its dealings with its public servants, who happen to be sanitation workers. Now, we've got to keep attention on that....

Now we're going to march again, and we've got to march again, in order to put the issue where it is supposed to be. And force everybody to see that there are thirteen hundred of God's children here suffering.... That's the issue. And we've got to say to the nation: we know it's coming out. For when people get caught up with that which is right and they are willing to sacrifice for it, there is no stopping point short of victory.

We aren't going to let any mace stop us. We are masters in our nonviolent movement in disarming police forces; they don't know what to do.... I remember in Birmingham, Alabama, when we were in that majestic struggle there we would move out of the 16th Street Baptist Church day after day; by the hundreds we would move out. And [Sheriff] Bull Connor would tell them to send the dogs forth and they did come; but we just went before the dogs singing, "Ain't gonna let nobody turn me round." Bull Connor next would say, "Turn the fire hoses on...." [But] Bull Connor didn't know history.... [He didn't know] that there was a certain kind of fire that no water could put out....

That couldn't stop us. And we just went on before the dogs and we would look at them; and we'd go on before the water hoses and we would look at it, and we'd just go on singing, "Over my head I see freedom in the air." And then we would be thrown in the **paddy wagons....** Old Bull would say, "Take them off," and they did; and we would just go in the paddy wagon singing, "We Shall Overcome." And every now and then we'd get in the jail, and we'd see the jailers looking through the windows being moved by our prayers, and being moved by our words and our songs. And there was a power there which Bull Connor couldn't adjust to; and so we ended up transforming Bull into a steer, and we won our struggle in Birmingham.

Now we've got to go on to Memphis just like that....

We need all of you. And you know what's beautiful to me, is to see all of these ministers of the Gospel.... Who is it that is supposed to articulate the longings and aspirations of the people more than the preacher? Somehow the preacher must be an Amos, and say, "Let justice roll down like waters and righteousness like a mighty stream." Somehow, the preacher must say with Jesus, "The spirit of the Lord is upon me, because he hath anointed me to deal with the problems of the poor."

And I want to commend the preachers.... I want to thank them all. And I want you to thank them, because so often, preachers aren't concerned about anything but themselves. And I'm always happy to see a **relevant** ministry.

paddy wagons: special police vehicles for transporting prisoners.

relevant: having a significant impact on or relationship to the matter at hand.

It's alright to talk about "long white robes over yonder," in all of its symbolism. But ultimately people want some suits and dresses and shoes to wear down here. It's alright to talk about "streets flowing with milk and honey," but God has commanded us to be concerned about the slums down here, and his children who can't eat three square meals a day. It's alright to talk about the new Jerusalem, but one day, God's preacher must talk about the New York, the new Atlanta, the new Philadelphia, the new Los Angeles, the new Memphis, Tennessee. This is what we have to do.

Now the other thing we'll have to do is this: Always anchor our external direct action with the power of economic withdrawal. Now, we are poor people, individually, we are poor when you compare us with white society in America.... [But] never stop and forget that collectively, that means all of us together, collectively we are richer than all the nations in the world, with the exception of nine.... That's power right there, if we know how to pool it.

We don't have to argue with anybody. We don't have to curse and go around acting bad with our words. We don't need any bricks and bottles, we don't need any Molotov cocktails, we just need to go around to these stores, and to these massive industries in our country, and say, "God sent us by here, to say to you that you're not treating his children right. And we've come by here to ask you to make the first item on your agenda—fair treatment, where God's children are concerned. Now, if you are not prepared to do that, we do have an agenda that we must follow. And our agenda calls for withdrawing economic support from you."

And so, as a result of this, we are asking you tonight, to go out and tell your neighbors not to buy Coca-Cola in Memphis. Go by and tell them not to buy Sealtest milk. Tell them not to buy—what is the other bread?—Wonder Bread. And what is the other bread company, Jesse? Tell them not to buy Hart's bread. As Jesse Jackson has said, up to now, only the garbage men have been feeling pain; now we must kind of **redistribute** the pain. We are choosing these companies because they haven't been fair in their hiring policies; and we are choosing them because they can begin the process of saying, they are going to support the needs and the rights of

redistribute: spread around more equally.

Martin Luther King, Jr.

these men who are on strike. And then they can move on downtown and tell [the mayor] to do what is right.

But not only that, we've got to strengthen black institutions. I call upon you to take your money out of the banks downtown and deposit your money in Tri-State Bank—we want a "bank-in" movement in Memphis.... You have six or seven black insurance companies in Memphis. Take out your insurance there. We want to have an "insurance-in."

Now these are some practical things we can do. We begin the process of building a greater economic base. And at the same time, we are putting pressure where it really hurts. I ask you to follow through here.

Now, let me say as I move to my conclusion that we've got to give ourselves to this struggle until the end. Nothing would be more tragic than to stop at this point, in Memphis. We've got to see it through. And when we have our march, you need to be there. Be concerned about your brother. You may not be on strike. But either we go up together, or we go down together.

Let us develop a kind of dangerous unselfishness. One day a man came to Jesus; and he wanted to raise some questions about some vital matters in life. At points, he wanted to trick Jesus, and show him that he knew a little more than Jesus knew, and through this, throw him off base.

Now that question could have easily ended up in a philosophical and **theological** debate. But Jesus immediately pulled that question from mid-air, and placed it on a dangerous curve between Jerusalem and Jericho. And he talked about a certain man, who fell among thieves. You remember that a **Levite** and a priest passed by on the other side. They didn't stop to help him. And finally a man of another race came by. He got down from his beast..., administered first aid, and helped the man in need. Jesus ended up saying, this was the good man, this was the great man, because he had the capacity to project the "I" into the "thou," and to be concerned about his brother.

Now you know, we use our imagination a great deal to try to determine why the priest and the Levite didn't stop. At times we say they were busy going to church meetings ... and they had to get on down to Jerusalem so they wouldn't be

theological: characterized by the study of religious faith and practice.

Levite: a member of the priestly Hebrew tribe of Levi.

late for their meeting. At other times we would speculate that there was a religious law that "one who was engaged in religious ceremonials was not to touch a human body twenty-four hours before the ceremony." And every now and then we begin to wonder whether maybe they were not going down to Jerusalem, or down to Jericho, rather to organize a "Jericho Road Improvement Association." That's a possibility. Maybe they felt that it was better to deal with the problem from the causal root, rather than to get bogged down with an individual effort.

But I'm going to tell you what my imagination tells me. It's possible that these men were afraid. You see, the Jericho road is a dangerous road. I remember when Mrs. King and I were first in Jerusalem. We rented a car and drove from Jerusalem down to Jericho. And as soon as we got on that road, I said to my wife, "I can see why Jesus used this as a setting for his **parable**." It's a winding, meandering road. It's really **conducive** for ambushing.... In the days of Jesus it came to be known as the "Bloody Pass." And you know, it's possible that the priest and the Levite looked over that man on the ground and wondered if the robbers were still around. Or it's possible that they felt that the man on the ground was merely faking. And he was acting like he had been robbed and hurt, in order to seize them over there.... And so the first question that the Levite asked was, "If I stop to help this man, what will happen to me?" But then the Good Samaritan came by. And he reversed the question: "If I do not stop to help this man, what will happen to him?"

That's the question before you tonight. Not, "If I stop to help the sanitation workers, what will happen to all of the hours that I usually spend in my office every day and every week as a pastor?" The question is not, "If I stop to help this man in need, what will happen to me?" "If I do not stop to help the sanitation workers, what will happen to them?" That's the question.

Let us rise up tonight with greater readiness. Let us stand with a greater determination. And let us move on in these powerful days, these days of challenge to make America what it ought to be. We have an opportunity to make America a better nation. And I want to thank God, once more, for allowing me to be here with you.

parable: story, lesson (usually religious or moral).

conducive: tending to encourage or help.

Martin Luther King, Jr.

You know, several years ago [in 1958], I was in New York City autographing the first book that I had written. And while sitting there autographing books, a demented black woman came up.... Before I knew it I had been stabbed by this demented woman. I was rushed to Harlem Hospital.... That blade had gone through, and the x-rays revealed that the tip of the blade was on the edge of my aorta, the main artery. And once that's punctured, you drown in your own blood—that's the end of you.

It came out in the *New York Times* the next morning, that if I had sneezed, I would have died. Well, about four days later, they allowed me ... to move around in the wheelchair in the hospital. They allowed me to read some of the mail that came in.... I read a few [of the letters], but one of them I will never forget.... [It was] from a little girl.... It said simply, "Dear Dr. King: I am a ninth-grade student at the White Plains High School." She said, "While it should not matter, I would like to mention that I am a white girl. I read in the paper of your misfortune, and of your suffering. And I read that if you had sneezed, you would have died. And I'm simply writing you to say that I'm so happy that you didn't sneeze."

And I want to say tonight ... that I am happy that I didn't sneeze. Because if I had sneezed, I wouldn't have been around here in 1960, when students all over the South started sitting-in at lunch counters. And I knew that as they were sitting in, they were really standing up for the best in the American dream....

If I had sneezed, I wouldn't have been around in 1962, when Negroes in Albany, Georgia, decided to straighten their backs up. And whenever men and women straighten their backs up, they are going somewhere, because a man can't ride your back unless it is bent.

If I had sneezed, I wouldn't have been here in 1963, when the black people of Birmingham, Alabama, aroused the conscience of this nation, and brought into being the Civil Rights Bill.

If I had sneezed, I wouldn't have had a chance later that year, in August, to try to tell America about a dream that I had had.

If I had sneezed, I wouldn't have been down in Selma, Alabama, to see the great movement there.

If I had sneezed, I wouldn't have been in Memphis to see a community rally around those brothers and sisters who are suffering.

I'm so happy that I didn't sneeze....

It really doesn't matter what happens now. I left Atlanta this morning, and as we got started on the plane, there were six of us, the pilot said over the public address system, "We are sorry for the delay but we have Dr. Martin Luther King on the plane. And to be sure that all of the bags were checked, and to be sure that nothing would be wrong with the plane, we had to check out everything carefully. And we've had the plane protected and guarded all night."

And then I got into Memphis. And some began to say the threats, or talk about the threats that were out. What would happen to me from some of our sick white brothers?

Well, I don't know what will happen now. We've got some difficult days ahead. But it doesn't matter with me now.

Martin Luther King, Jr.

Because I've been to the mountaintop. And I don't mind. Like anybody, I would like to live a long life.... But I'm not concerned about that now. I just want to do God's will. And He's allowed me to go up to the mountain. And I've looked over. And I've seen the promised land. I may not get there with you. But I want you to know tonight, that we, as a people will get to the promised land. And I'm happy, tonight. I'm not worried about anything. I'm not fearing any man. Mine eyes have seen the glory of the coming of the Lord.

"

The very next day—April 4, 1968—King was struck down by an assassin's bullet as he stood on the balcony of his Memphis motel room.

Sources

Books

Bosmajian, Haig A., and Hamida Bosmajian, *The Rhetoric of the Civil Rights Movement,* Random House, 1969.

Boulware, Marcus H., *The Oratory of Negro Leaders: 1900-1968,* Negro Universities Press, 1969.

Branch, Taylor, *Parting the Waters: America in the King Years, 1954-1963,* Simon and Schuster, 1989.

Carson, Clayborne and others, editors, *The Eyes on the Prize Civil Rights Reader,* Penguin, 1991.

Duffy, Bernard K., and Halford R. Ryan, editors, *American Orators of the Twentieth Century: Critical Studies and Sources,* Greenwood Press, 1987.

Foner, Philip S., editor, *The Voice of Black America: Major Speeches by Negroes in the United States, 1797-1971,* Simon & Schuster, 1972.

Hill, Roy L., *Rhetoric of Racial Revolt,* Golden Bell Press, 1964.

Holland, DeWitte, editor, *America in Controversy: History of American Public Address,* William C. Brown Company, 1973.

King, Coretta Scott, *My Life with Martin Luther King, Jr.,* Holt, 1969.

King, Martin Luther, Jr., *Stride toward Freedom: The Montgomery Story,* Harper & Row, 1958.

King, Martin Luther, Jr., *Strength to Love,* Harper & Row, 1963.

King, Martin Luther, Jr., *The Papers of Martin Luther King, Jr.,* edited by Clayborne Carson and Ralph E. Luker, Volume 1: *Called to Serve, January 1929–June 1951,* University of California, 1992. [Set is projected to run fourteen volumes when completed.]

Lewis, David L., *King: A Biography,* second edition, University of Illinois Press, 1978.

Oates, Stephen B., *Let the Trumpet Sound: The Life of Martin Luther King, Jr.,* New American Library, 1982.

O'Neill, Daniel J., editor, *Speeches by Black Americans,* Dickenson Publishing Company, 1971.

O'Neill, William L., *Coming Apart: An Informal History of America in the 1960s,* Quadrangle, 1971.

Scott, Robert L., and Wayne Brockriede, *The Rhetoric of Black Power,* Harper & Row, 1969.

Smith, Arthur L., and Stephen Robb, editors, *The Voice of Black Rhetoric: Selections,* Allyn & Bacon, 1971.

Washington, James Melvin, *A Testament of Hope: The Essential Writings of Martin Luther King, Jr.,* Harper & Row, 1986.

Periodicals

Commonweal, "Doctor King's Legacy," April 19, 1968, pp. 125-126.

Ebony, "I've Been to the Mountaintop," May 1968; "Prince of Peace Is Dead," May 1968.

Freedomways, spring, 1967, pp. 103-117.

Liberation, January 1965, pp. 28-29.

Newsweek, April 15, 1968, pp. 34-38; "King's Last March: We Lost Somebody," April 22, 1968, pp. 26-31.

New York Times, April 5, 1968.

Time, April 12, 1968, pp. 18-21; "King's Last March," April 19, 1968, pp. 18-19.

Worldview, "New Sense of Direction," April 1972.

Malcolm X

1925–1965

Religious leader and activist

Malcolm X was the chief spokesman of the Nation of Islam during the late 1950s and early 1960s. A controversial and often feared figure, especially among whites, he met a sudden and violent end at the hands of several assassins during a turbulent period of American history. Yet more than thirty years after his death, Malcolm X is a powerful symbol of black pride whose words continue to inspire a new generation.

Early Life

Malcolm X was born Malcolm Little in Omaha, Nebraska, one of eight children of Louise Norton Little and Earl Little, a Baptist minister. Earl Little was a follower of **Marcus Garvey** *(see entry)*, an African American leader of the early nineteenth century who proposed that blacks separate from white society and return to Africa to establish their own nation. Holding such radical beliefs made Earl Little the target of various white vigilante groups, and their threats

"I'M NONVIOLENT WITH THOSE WHO ARE NONVIOLENT WITH ME. BUT WHEN YOU DROP THAT VIOLENCE ON ME, THEN YOU'VE MADE ME GO INSANE, AND I'M NOT RESPONSIBLE FOR WHAT I DO...."

"YOU LET THAT WHITE MAN KNOW, IF THIS IS A COUNTRY OF FREEDOM, LET IT BE A COUNTRY OF FREEDOM; AND IF IT'S NOT A COUNTRY OF FREEDOM, CHANGE IT."

eventually forced the family to flee to Milwaukee, Wisconsin, and from there to Lansing, Michigan.

In Michigan, however, the Littles experienced even more harassment. In 1929 their house was burned to the ground by a white terrorist group. And in 1931, Earl Little himself was found dead on some streetcar tracks. The police called it an accident, but the family suspected it was really murder.

By the late 1930s, the years of turmoil and tragedy proved too much for Louise Little to bear. No longer able to care for herself or her children, she was committed to a mental hospital. Government officials then arranged for Malcolm and his **siblings** to live in foster homes and state institutions.

Despite this upheaval in his life, young Malcolm was an excellent student and class leader who dreamed one day of becoming a lawyer. But after one of his teachers pointed out to him that as a black he should aim for a profession more in keeping with his place in society (such as carpentry, the teacher suggested), he lost interest in school and soon dropped out.

Becomes a Follower of Elijah Muhammad

Malcolm then headed to Boston, Massachusetts and worked at a series of menial jobs and committed a few petty crimes. From there he moved to Harlem, a borough in New York City with a large African American population. There, as a streetwise hustler nicknamed "Detroit Red," he became involved in gambling, selling drugs, and prostitution. Malcolm then returned to Boston and headed a burglary ring. In 1946, his criminal activities landed him in prison.

While serving his time, Malcolm—nicknamed "Satan" by his fellow inmates because he was so full of anger and hate—took steps to turn his life around through a process of self-education.

During this period Malcolm embraced the teachings of Elijah Muhammad, the spiritual leader of the Nation of Islam, or, as the group was frequently called at that time, the Black Muslims, a black separatist movement that had been established in the United States during the 1930s by a

siblings: brothers and sisters.

mysterious traveling salesman named W. D. Fard (also known as Wali Farad or Wallace Fard Muhammad). Black Muslims reject Christianity as a white man's religion. Their system of belief blends **black nationalism** with their own interpretation of Islam, the religion founded by the Prophet Muhammad in the seventh century and practiced today by about 935 million Muslims worldwide. Black Muslims believe that blacks are descended from a superior race of African and Asian Muslims, and are God's chosen people. Other teachings of the Nation of Islam emphasize achieving economic independence and showing respect for black women. In addition, Black Muslims strictly forbid eating pork and using alcohol and drugs. They also strongly disapprove of gambling, stealing, sex outside of marriage, and "frivolous" activities such as dancing or going to the movies. [See box on page 229 for more information.]

As part of his conversion to the Nation of Islam, Malcolm dropped the "slave name" Little to take on the surname "X" as a symbol of the unknown African name of his ancestors. After being paroled in 1952, he set out to meet Elijah Muhammad so that he could express his devotion in person. The spiritual leader was very impressed, and quickly accepted Malcolm X into the Nation of Islam and made him a minister.

Achieves National Recognition

Throughout the rest of the 1950s and into the early 1960s, Malcolm X served at **mosques** in Detroit, Philadelphia, and Harlem. In addition, he frequently traveled throughout the country helping to establish new congregations in other cities with fairly large black populations. His forceful personality and spellbinding public speaking skills soon transformed the Nation of Islam from a relatively minor religious group into a nationwide force of perhaps ten thousand official members and countless others who more or less supported their goals.

In a typical speech from this period—before he had attracted much national attention—Malcolm X focused mostly on explaining the beliefs of Elijah Muhammad and the Nation of Islam. He denounced whites as "devils" and

black nationalism: the belief that blacks should separate from whites to form their own self-governing communities and businesses.

mosques: Islamic houses of worship.

predicted that the world as they knew it would soon end. He also condemned integration, interracial marriage, and mainstream political and social movements, including the civil rights movement and its leaders. On the other hand, he praised the concept of black nationalism, black self-discipline and self-determination, and black unity.

Malcolm X's role as the Nation of Islam's most visible and effective spokesman soon made him a popular guest on college campuses, at meetings of various associations, and on radio and television programs. But as his audience broadened, he spent less time repeating Elijah Muhammad and explaining Black Muslim theology. Instead, he talked about everyday concerns that were of greater interest to him personally—racism, politics, economics, justice, human rights. His tone became angrier, more militant, and full of biting sarcasm. Especially alarming to some people was that he began urging blacks to take up arms in self-defense against hostile whites. Many believed that the fierce young leader—who was successfully stirring up thousands of working-class blacks—was trying to provoke a violent race war. The media helped reinforce this idea by always portraying Malcolm X as a dangerous outlaw and rabble-rouser.

Meanwhile, tensions were building within the Nation of Islam itself. Elijah Muhammad and other Black Muslim leaders had begun to doubt the depth of Malcolm X's commitment to their faith, especially when they saw him turn away from certain aspects of it that were somewhat cult-like. They were also suspicious of the publicity Malcolm X attracted wherever he went.

The situation finally came to a head in late 1963. Following the assassination of President John F. Kennedy on November 22, Malcolm X shocked and angered many people when he described the killing as a case of "chickens coming home to roost" in a society that tolerated white violence against blacks. (His use of that expression implied that he felt the president had gotten what he deserved.) Elijah Muhammad responded to the public outcry that greeted this remark by ending Malcolm X's role as the Nation's chief spokesman.

The standoff between Malcolm X and Elijah Muhammad continued until March 12, 1964, when Malcolm X

The Development of the Nation of Islam

The Nation of Islam was established in the United States during the 1930s by a mysterious traveling salesman named W. D. Fard (also Wali Farad/) or Wallace Fard Muhammad. Fard used his own mythological interpretation of the Bible to convince many Africans Americans that Islam and not Christianity was the religion of black people in Africa and Asia. When he developed a large following, he rented a hall, calling it the Temple of Islam. Those who wished to join the temple were first required to apply for Islamic names to replace the slave names the white man had given them.

One of Fard's most devoted followers was a former Detroit autoworker named Elijah Muhammad. After Fard mysteriously disappeared in 1934, Elijah Muhammad became the Nation's new spiritual leader, remaining head of the movement until his death in 1975. Muhammad built a second temple in Chicago and transformed the movement under his own intense and militant leadership. Because he believed that whites had created the poor economic conditions that caused blacks to suffer, to Muhammad, separation from the white race was the only solution. He urged blacks to reclaim the land their parents and ancestors had paid for with their toil and sacrifice throughout 300 years of slavery. He fought for the economic and social advancement of his followers and promoted self-improvement, health, and abstinence from cigarettes and alcohol. He also instilled black pride and brotherhood. Muhammad is often credited as the one person most responsible for taking the word "Negro" out of the everyday American vocabulary and replacing it with "black person."

The Nation of Islam included about 8,000 members when Muhammad took it over and it grew rapidly under his leadership. Muhammad differed from Fard in his emphases: while Fard stressed the mythological basis of Black Muslims, Muhammad worked toward building a strong economic base. Under his direction, the Nation accumulated a great deal of real estate including farms and rental property, a newspaper, local businesses such as a supermarket and bakeries, and an interest in a bank.

announced his intention to quit the Nation of Islam and form a new religious movement of his own, the Muslim Mosque, Inc. A short time later, he established another group, the Organization of Afro-American Unity. It was open to all blacks, regardless of their religious beliefs.

That same spring, on April 3, Malcolm X made a visit to Cleveland, Ohio. There he delivered what is perhaps his most famous speech, one he himself called "The Ballot or the Bullet." It brought together many of the themes he had been developing for some time. With only slight changes to *suit different audiences or different locations, it soon became his standard speech. The following excerpt is taken from* Malcolm X Speaks: Selected Speeches and Statements, *edited by George Breitman, published by Pathfinder Press, 1965.*

66

Mr. Moderator, Brother Lomax, brothers and sisters, friends and enemies: I just can't believe everyone in here is a friend and I don't want to leave anybody out. The question tonight, as I understand it, is "The Negro Revolt, and Where Do We Go From Here?" or "What Next?" In my little humble way of understanding it, it points toward either the ballot or the bullet....

I'm not here tonight to discuss my religion. I'm not here to try and change your religion. I'm not here to argue or discuss anything that we differ about, because it's time for us to submerge our differences and realize that it is best for us to first see that we have the same problem, a common problem—a problem that will make you catch hell whether you're a Baptist, or a Methodist, or a Muslim, or a nationalist. Whether you're educated or illiterate, whether you live on the boulevard or in the alley, you're going to catch hell just like I am. We're all in the same boat and we all are going to catch the same hell from the same man. He just happens to be a white man....

Now in speaking like this, it doesn't mean that we're anti-white, but it does mean we're anti-exploitation, we're anti-degradation, we're anti-oppression. And if the white man doesn't want us to be anti-him, let him stop oppressing and exploiting and degrading us....

If we don't do something real soon, I think you'll have to agree that we're going to be forced either to use the ballot or the bullet. It's one or the other in 1964. It isn't that time is running out—time has run out! Nineteen-sixty-four threatens to be the most explosive year America has ever witnessed.... Why? It's also a political year. It's the year when all of the white politicians will be back in the so-called Negro community jiving you and me for some votes. The year when all of the white political crooks will be right back in your and my community with their false promises.... As they nourish these dissatisfactions, it can only lead to one thing, an explosion; and now we have the type of black man on the scene in America today ... who just doesn't intend to turn the other cheek any longer....

I'm not a politician, not even a student of politics; in fact, I'm not a student of much of anything. I'm not a Democrat, I'm not a Republican, and I don't even consider myself an American. If you and I were Americans, there'd be no problem.... Everything that came out of Europe, every blue-eyed thing, is already an American. And as long as you and I have been over here, we aren't Americans yet.

Well, I am one who doesn't believe in **deluding** myself. I'm not going to sit at your table and watch you eat, with nothing on my plate, and call myself a diner. Sitting at the table doesn't make you a diner, unless you eat some of what's on that plate. Being here in America doesn't make you an American. Being born here in America doesn't make you an American. Why, if birth made you American, you wouldn't need any legislation, you wouldn't need any amendments to the Constitution....

No, I'm not an American. I'm one of the twenty-two million black people who are the victims of Americanism. One of the twenty-two million black people who are the victims of democracy, nothing but disguised **hypocrisy**.... I'm speaking as a victim of this American system. And I see America through the eyes of the victim. I don't see any American dream; I see an American nightmare.

These twenty-two million victims are waking up.... They're becoming politically mature. They are realizing that there are new political trends from coast to coast. As they see these new political trends, it's possible for them to see that every time there's an election the races are so close that they have to have a recount.... Well, what does this mean? It means that when white people are evenly divided, and black people have a bloc of votes of their own, it is left up to them to determine who's going to sit in the White House and who's going to be in the dog house.

It was the black man's vote that put the present [Democratic] administration in Washington, D.C. Your vote, your

deluding: fooling.

hypocrisy: pretending to have high moral standards but not really living by them.

Malcolm X addresses a rally at Harlem

dumb vote, your ignorant vote, your wasted vote put in an administration in Washington, D.C., that has seen fit to pass every kind of legislation imaginable, saving you until last, then **filibustering** on top of that. And your and my leaders have the **audacity** to run around clapping their hands and talk about how much progress we're making....

So it's time in 1964 to wake up. And when you see them coming up with that kind of conspiracy, let them know your eyes are open. And let them know you got something else that's wide open too. It's got to be the ballot or the bullet. The ballot or the bullet. If you're afraid to use an expression like that, you should get on out of the country, you should get back in the cotton patch, you should get back in the alley. They get all the Negro vote, and after they get it, the Negro gets nothing in return. All they did when they got to Washington was give a few big Negroes big jobs. Those big Negroes didn't need big jobs, they already had jobs. That's camouflage, that's trickery, that's treachery, window-dressing. I'm not trying to knock out the Democrats for the Republi-

filibustering: using extreme delaying tactics to prevent a legislature from taking action on a bill.

audacity: nerve.

cans, we'll get to them in a minute. But it is true—you put the Democrats first and the Democrats put you last.

Look at it the way it is. What alibis do they use, since they control Congress and the Senate? What alibi do they use when you and I ask, "Well, when are you going to keep your promise?" They blame the Dixiecrats. What is a Dixiecrat? A Democrat. A Dixiecrat is nothing but a Democrat in disguise....

The Dixiecrats in Washington, D.C., control the key committees that run the government. The only reason the Dixiecrats control these committees is because they have seniority. The only reason they have seniority is because they come from states where Negroes can't vote. This is not even a government that's based on democracy. It is not a government that is made up of representatives of the people. Half of the people in the South can't even vote.... Half of the senators and congressmen who occupy these key positions in Washington, D.C., are there illegally, are there unconstitutionally....

If the black man in these Southern states had his full voting rights, the key Dixiecrats in Washington, D.C., which means the key Democrats in Washington, D.C., would lose their seats. The Democratic party itself would lose its power. It would cease to be powerful as a party....

I say again, I'm not anti-Democrat, I'm not anti-Republican, I'm not anti-anything. I'm just questioning their sincerity, and some of the strategy that they've been using on our people by promising them promises that they don't intend to keep.... That's why, in 1964, it's time now for you and me to become more politically mature and realize what the ballot is for; what we're supposed to get when we cast a ballot; and that if we don't cast a ballot, it's going to end up in a situation where we're going to have to cast a bullet. It's either a ballot or a bullet.

In the North, they do it a different way. They have a system that's known as gerrymandering, whatever that means. It means when Negroes become too heavily concentrated in a certain area, and begin to gain too much political power, the white man comes along and changes the district lines....

So, what I'm trying to impress upon you, in essence, is this: You and I in America are faced not with a segregationist conspiracy, we're faced with a government conspiracy.... You don't have anybody putting blocks in your path but people who are a part of the government. The same government that you go abroad to fight for and die for is the government that is in a conspiracy to deprive you of your voting rights, deprive you of your economic opportunities, deprive you of decent housing, deprive you of decent education.... The government of America ... is responsible for the oppression and exploitation and degradation of black people in this country. And you should drop it in their lap. This government has failed the Negro. This so-called democracy has failed the Negro. And all these white liberals have definitely failed the Negro.

So, where do we go from here? First, we need some friends. We need some new allies. The entire civil rights struggle needs a new interpretation, a broader interpretation. We need to look at this civil rights thing from another angle— from the inside as well as from the outside. To those of us whose philosophy is black nationalism, the only way you can get involved in the civil rights struggle is give it a new interpretation. That old interpretation excluded us.... These handkerchief-heads who have been dillydallying and pussyfooting and compromising—we don't intend to let them pussyfoot and dillydally and compromise any longer.

How can you thank a man for giving you what's already yours? How then can you thank him for giving you only part of what's already yours? You haven't even made progress, if what's being given to you, you should have had already. That's not progress....

And now you're facing a situation where the young Negro's coming up. They don't want to hear that "turn-the-other-cheek" stuff.... There's new strategy coming in. It'll be Molotov cocktails this month, hand grenades next month, and something else next month. It'll be ballots, or it'll be bullets. It'll be liberty, or it will be death....

The black nationalists, those whose philosophy is black nationalism, in bringing about this new interpretation of the entire meaning of civil rights, look upon it as meaning ... equality of opportunity. Well, we're justified in seeking civil rights, if it means equality of opportunity, because all we're doing there is trying to collect for our investment. Our mothers and fathers invested sweat and blood. Three hundred and ten years we worked in this country without a dime in return.... You let the white man walk around here talking about how rich this country is, but you never stop to think how it got rich so quick. It got rich because you made it rich....

Not only did we give of our free labor, we gave of our blood. Every time he had a call to arms, we were the first ones in uniform. We died on every battlefield the white man had. We have made a greater sacrifice than anybody who's standing up in America today. We have made a greater contribution and have collected less. Civil rights, for those of us whose philosophy is black nationalism, means: "Give it to us now. Don't wait for next year. Give it to us yesterday, and that's not fast enough."...

If you don't take this kind of stand, your little children will grow up and look at you and think "shame." If you don't take an **uncompromising** stand—I don't mean go out and get violent; but at the same time you should never be nonviolent unless you run into some nonviolence. I'm nonviolent with those who are nonviolent with me. But when you drop that violence on me, then you've made me go insane, and I'm not responsible for what I do. And that's the way every Negro should get. Any time you know you're within the law, within your legal rights, within your moral rights, in accord with justice, then die for what you believe in. But don't die alone. Let your dying be reciprocal. This is what is meant by equality....

When we begin to get in this area, we need new friends, we need new allies. We need to expand the civil rights strug-

uncompromising: firm.

gle to a higher level—to the level of human rights.... Civil rights means you're asking Uncle Sam to treat you right. Human rights are something you were born with. Human rights are your God-given rights. Human rights are the rights that are recognized by all nations of this earth. And any time any one violates your human rights, you can take them to the world court. Uncle Sam's hands are dripping with blood, dripping with the blood of the black man in this country. He's the earth's number-one hypocrite. He has the audacity—yes, he has—imagine him posing as the leader of the free world. The free world!—and you over here singing "We Shall Overcome"....

Let the world know how bloody his hands are. Let the world know the hypocrisy that's practiced over here. Let it be the ballot or the bullet. Let him know that it must be the ballot or the bullet....

By ballot I only mean freedom. Don't you know ... that the ballot is more important than the dollar? Can I prove it? Yes. Look in the U[nited] N[ations]. There are poor nations in the UN; yet those poor nations can get together with their voting power and keep the rich nations from making a move. They have one nation—one vote, everyone has an equal vote. And when those brothers from Asia, and Africa and the darker parts of this earth get together, their voting power is sufficient to hold Sam in check. Or Russia in check. Or some other section of the earth in check. So, the ballot is most important.

Right now, in this country, if you and I, twenty-two million African Americans—that's what we are—Africans who are in America. You're nothing but Africans. Nothing but Africans. In fact, you'd get farther calling yourself African instead of Negro. Africans don't catch hell. You're the only one catching hell. They don't have to pass civil rights bills for Africans. An African can go anywhere he wants right now. All you've got to do is tie your head up. That's right, go anywhere you want. Just stop being a Negro. Change your name to Hoogagagooba. That'll show you how silly the white man is....

You're dealing with a man whose bias and prejudice are making him lose his mind, his intelligence, every day. He's frightened. He looks around and sees what's taking place on

this earth, and he sees that the pendulum of time is swinging in your direction. The dark people are waking up. They're losing their fear of the white man.... You've got to be mighty naive, or you've got to play the black man cheap, if you don't think some day he's going to wake up and find that it's got to be the ballot or the bullet....

The political philosophy of black nationalism means that the black man should control the politics and the politicians in his own community; no more. The black man in the black community has to be re-educated into the science of politics so he will know what politics is supposed to bring him in return. Don't be throwing out any ballots. A ballot is like a bullet. You don't throw your ballots until you see a target, and if that target is not within your reach, keep your ballot in your pocket.... Black people are fed up with the dillydallying, pussyfooting, compromising approach that we've been using toward getting our freedom. We want freedom now, but we're not going to get it saying "We Shall Overcome." We've got to fight until we overcome.

Malcolm X at a Nation of Islam gathering

The economic philosophy of black nationalism is pure and simple. It only means that we should control the economy of our community.... Our people have to be made to see that any time you take your dollar out of your community and spend it in a community where you don't live, the community where you live will get poorer and poorer, and the community where you spend your money will get richer and richer. Then you wonder why where you live is always a ghetto or a slum area....

The social philosophy of black nationalism only means that we have to get together and remove the evils, the vices, alcoholism, drug addiction, and other evils that are destroying the moral fiber of our community. We ourselves have to lift the level of our community, the standard of our community to a higher level, make our own society beautiful so that we will be satisfied in our own social circles and won't be running around here trying to knock our way into a social circle where we're not wanted.

So I say, in spreading a gospel such as black nationalism, it is not designed to make the black man re-evaluate the white man—you know him already—but to make the black man re-evaluate himself. Don't change the white man's mind—you can't change his mind, and that whole thing about appealing to the moral conscience of America—America's conscience is **bankrupt....** You're wasting your time appealing to the moral conscience of a bankrupt man like Uncle Sam. If he had a conscience, he'd straighten this thing out with no more pressure being put upon him.... We've got to change our own minds about each other. We have to see each other with new eyes. We have to see each other as brothers and sisters. We have to come together with warmth so we can develop unity and harmony that's necessary to get this problem solved ourselves. How can we do this? How can we avoid jealousy? How can we avoid the suspicion and the divisions that exist in the community? I'll tell you how....

Our gospel is black nationalism. We're not trying to threaten the existence of any organization, but we're spreading the gospel of black nationalism. Anywhere there's a church that is also preaching and practicing the gospel of black nationalism, join that church. If the NAACP [National Association for the Advancement of Colored People] is preaching and prac-

bankrupt: lacking any valuable qualities.

Malcolm X

ticing the gospel of black nationalism, join the NAACP. If CORE [Congress of Racial Equality] is spreading and practicing the gospel of black nationalism, join CORE. Join any organization that has a gospel that's for the uplift of the black man. And when you get into it and see them pussyfooting or compromising, pull out of it because that's not black nationalism. We'll find another one.

And in this manner, the organizations will increase in number and in quantity and in quality, and by August, it is then our intention to have a black nationalist convention which will consist of delegates from all over the country who are interested in the political, economic and social philosophy of black nationalism.... We want to hear new ideas and new solutions and new answers. And at that time, if we see fit then to form a black nationalist party, we'll form a black nationalist party. If it's necessary to form a black nationalist army, we'll form a black nationalist army. It'll be the ballot or the bullet. It'll be liberty or it'll be death.

It's time for you and me to stop sitting in this country, letting some **cracker** senators, Northern crackers and Southern crackers, sit there in Washington, D.C., and come to a conclusion in their mind that you and I are supposed to have civil rights. There's no white man going to tell me anything about my rights. Brothers and sisters, always remember, if it doesn't take senators and congressmen and presidential proclamations to give freedom to the white man, it is not necessary for legislation or proclamation or Supreme Court decisions to give freedom to the black man. You let that white man know, if this is a country of freedom, let it be a country of freedom; and if it's not a country of freedom, change it.

We will work with anybody, anywhere, at any time, who is genuinely interested in tackling the problem head-on, nonviolently as long as the enemy is nonviolent, but violent when the enemy gets violent. We'll work with you on the voter-registration drive, we'll work with you on rent strikes, we'll work with you on school boycotts—I don't believe in any kind of integration; I'm not even worried about it because I know you're not going to get it anyway; you're not going to get it because you're afraid to die; you've got to be ready to die if you try and force yourself on the white man....

cracker: an insulting term for a poor (usually Southern) white.

Louis Farrakhan, Nation of Islam Leader (1933–)

Louis Farrakhan, whose original name was Louis Eugene Walcott, was born in New York City in 1933. A good student and athlete who also enjoyed music and performing, he dropped out of college to seek his fortune in show business. He was working as a nightclub guitarist and calypso singer when Malcolm X personally recruited him into the Boston branch of the Nation of Islam.

Adopting the new name Louis Abdul Farrakhan, he quickly distinguished himself as a member of the Nation's security force and training unit for young men. Soon he was promoted to minister and served as an assistant to Malcolm X. When Elijah Muhammad transferred Malcolm X from Boston to Harlem, Farrakhan became head of the Boston mosque (temple). Then Malcolm X left the Nation in 1964, and Farrakhan eventually replaced him as head of the Harlem mosque, also assuming his role as Elijah Muhammad's top aide and chief spokesman of the Nation of Islam.

When Elijah Muhammad died in 1975, the Nation was in turmoil. Farrakhan clashed with Elijah Muhammad's son and designated successor, W. Deen Muhammad, who wanted to downplay the elements of black nationalism in his father's philosophy and observe a more traditional form of Islam. Farrakhan, on the other hand, urged Black Muslims to remain true to the vision of Elijah Muhammad. Finally,

in 1977 Farrakhan and a few thousand of his followers broke away from the group to reestablish the Nation of Islam in keeping with the teachings of Elijah Muhammad. He was becoming a well-known figure among urban blacks at this time, regularly filling stadiums and college auditoriums across the country for Nation of Islam rallies.

When Jesse Jackson entered the 1984 race for the Democratic presidential nomination, the Black Muslims broke with their practice of staying out of politics. Members of the group provided security for Jackson and his staff, and Farrakhan himself was seen at Jackson's side at many public events. This bothered many Democrats, especially Jewish ones who found many of Farrakhan's statements anti-Semitic (hostile to Jews). In early 1984 Jackson's campaign was severely damaged when it was reported that he had used ethnic slurs about Jews in a private conversation. Jackson apologized for his statements and began to distance himself from Farrakhan. Farrakhan publicly came to Jackson's defense, but his arguments were perceived by many as more anti-Semitism and racial hatred.

Through the next decade Farrakhan made headlines on several more occasions for anti-Semitic remarks. In addition, he raised eyebrows with a number of elaborate conspiracy theories, including claims that AIDS is part of a plot by the United States government to wipe out black Africans and that whites deliberately introduced guns and drugs into the nation's ghettos so that

African Americans would destroy themselves.

In 1993 Farrakhan seemed ready to make peace with those he had criticized in the past, reaching out to various Jewish leaders, to Coretta Scott King and other members of the Southern Christian Leadership Conference, and to the Congressional Black Caucus. Even his peacemaking activities, however, aroused controversy. Benjamin Chavis, then head of the National Association for the Advancement of Colored People (NAACP) invited him to attend a special political meeting involving several major black leaders. This gesture of cooperation disturbed many people who felt that the NAACP had no business associating Itself with the Nation of Islam. But the meeting went ahead as planned and ended with a declaration of unity between the mainstream black leaders and Farrakhan.

Later in 1993, Farrakhan spent weeks defending one of his top aides, Khallid Abdul Muhammad, who had delivered a viciously anti-Semitic, anti-Catholic, and anti-gay speech at a New Jersey college. Although he demoted Muhammad, Farrakhan proclaimed that he agreed with the "truth" of what his aide had said, if not the spirit in which he had said it. Later that month, he made a highly-publicized (and widely condemned) television appearance on *The Arsenio Hall Show*.

Farrakhan enjoyed a triumph at the end of 1995 with the success of the all-black

"Million Man March" in Washington, D.C. on October 16. As co-organizer of the event with Benjamin Chavis, his prestige among non-Muslim blacks reached an all-time high. Many who were uncomfortable with his previous messages of racial hatred praised him for trying to promote black self-help and self-discipline and for taking a strong moral stand against crime and drugs. Farrakhan made it very clear that he intended to be a part of the political mainstream. "I am a reality in America," he proclaimed. And as a *Time* correspondent once observed, "Love Farrakhan or hate him, the inescapable fact is that he touches a nerve among blacks as almost no one else can."

In the mid-1990s there were an estimated 20,000 members of the Nation of Islam.

You know the best way to get rid of segregation? The white man is more afraid of separation than he is of integration. Segregation means that he puts you away from him, but not far enough for you to be out of his jurisdiction; separation means you're gone. And the white man will integrate faster than he'll let you separate. So we will work with you against the segregated school system because it's criminal, because it is absolutely destructive, in every way imaginable, to the minds of the children who have to be exposed to that type of crippling education.

Last but not least, I must say this concerning the great controversy over rifles and shotguns. The only thing that I've ever said is that in areas where the government has proven itself either unwilling or unable to defend the lives and the property of Negroes, it's time for Negroes to defend themselves. Article number two of the constitutional amendments provides you and me the right to own a rifle or a shotgun.... This doesn't mean you're going to get a rifle and form battalions and go out looking for white folks, although you'd be within your rights—I mean, you'd be justified; but that would be illegal and we don't do anything illegal. If the white man doesn't want the black man buying rifles and shotguns, then let the government do its job....

This doesn't mean forming rifle clubs and going out looking for people, but it is time, in 1964, if you are a man, to let that man know. If he's not going to do his job in running the government and providing you and me with the protection that our taxes are supposed to be for, since he spends all those billions for his defense budget, he certainly can't begrudge you and me spending $12 or $15 for a single-shot, or double-action. I hope you understand. Don't go out shooting people, but any time ... you and I sit around and read where they bomb a church and murder in cold blood, not some grownups, but four little girls while they were praying to the same god the white man taught them to pray to, and you and I see the government go down and can't find who did it.

Why, this man—he can find [Nazi war criminal Adolf] Eichmann hiding down in Argentina somewhere. Let two or three American soldiers, who are minding somebody else's business way over in South Vietnam, get killed, and he'll send battleships, sticking his nose in their business. He wanted to send troops down to Cuba and make them have what he calls free elections—this old cracker who doesn't have free elections in his own country. No, if you never see me another time in your life, if I die in the morning, I'll die saying one thing: the ballot or the bullet, the ballot or the bullet.

If a Negro in 1964 has to sit around and wait for some cracker senator to filibuster when it comes to the rights of black people, why, you and I should hang our heads in shame. You talk about a march on Washington in 1963, you haven't seen anything. There's some more going down in '64. And this time they're not going like they went last year. They're not going singing "We Shall Overcome." They're not going with white friends. They're not going with placards already painted for them. They're not going with round-trip tickets. They're going with one-way tickets.

And if they don't want that non-nonviolent army going down there, tell them to bring the filibuster to a halt. The black nationalists aren't going to wait. Lyndon B. Johnson is the head of the Democratic Party. If he's for civil rights, let him go into the Senate next week and declare himself. Let him go in there right now and declare himself. Let him go in there and denounce the Southern branch of his party. Let him go in there right now and take a moral stand—right now, not later. Tell him, don't wait until election time. If he waits too long, brothers and sisters, he will be responsible for letting a condition develop in this country which will create a climate that will bring seeds up out of the ground with vegetation on the end of them looking like something these people never dreamed of. In 1964, it's the ballot or the bullet. Thank you.

99

Shortly after giving this speech, Malcolm X went to Mecca, the holy city of Islam. He then spent several months traveling and studying in the Middle East and Africa. The sight of people from all different races coming together in the name of Islam made a very strong impression on Malcolm X. Upon his return to the United States in late 1964, he declared himself to be a changed man. He announced his conversion to orthodox Islam and said that from then on he wanted to be known by the name of El-Hajj Malik El-Shabazz.

*Malcolm X's new outlook on life blended elements of his religious faith with **socialism, anticolonialism,** and what came to be known as "black consciousness"—the idea of creating a strong, separate identity for black people by emphasizing self-worth and self-reliance. In addition, he softened his views on a variety of issues and tried to down-play his fierce image. As part of that effort, he also began to reach out to the very people and movements he had condemned in the past, including moderate blacks and progressive whites.*

Meanwhile, relations between Malcolm X and Elijah Muhammad were very tense. Malcolm X charged his former teacher with scandalous behavior and harshly criticized the Nation of Islam. Spokesmen for Elijah Muhammad responded with insults and accusations of their own. Before long, Malcolm X reported receiving several death threats. During the middle of the night on February 14, 1965, he and his family were forced to flee from their home after a firebomb attack. Exactly one week later, Malcolm X was preparing to address some of his followers in Harlem's Audubon Ballroom when three black men with known connections to the Nation of Islam approached him. His pregnant wife and four daughters watched in horror as the men opened fire, striking Malcolm X more than a dozen times. He died a short time later. All three of the gunmen were convicted of his murder and sent to prison. Two have since been paroled.

In January 1995 one of Malcolm X's daughters, Qubilah Shabazz, was arrested and charged with trying to hire a man to kill the current head of the Nation of Islam, Louis Farrakhan (see box on pages 240–241). Members of the slain black leader's family (and many other people) suspected Farrakhan of somehow being involved in the assassination. Although Malcolm X had recruited Farrakhan into the Nation, the two men became bitter enemies. In fact, Farrakhan gave a number of speeches just before Malcolm X's death declaring that he was a traitor who deserved to

socialism: an economic and political system that involves government ownership and management of the means to produce and distribute goods.

anticolonialism: opposition to the practice of one country controlling another and making its people dependent on the country in power for help and support.

die. Farrakhan also replaced Malcolm X as head of the Harlem mosque and took over his role as Elijah Muhammad's top aide and chief spokesman of the Nation of Islam.

Farrakhan admits that his angry words about Malcolm X might have set the stage for violence, but he has always denied that he was behind any plot to do away with his rival.

Malcolm X has continued to powerfully inspire African Americans in the decades since his death. The Autobiography of Malcolm X, *which he and author* **Alex Haley** *(see entry) finished just days before his assassination, has been a steady best-seller for thirty years. In 1992 film director Spike Lee's blockbuster film,* Malcolm X *brought about an explosion of interest in a new generation of black Americans.*

Sources

Books

Bosmajian, Haig A., and Hamida Bosmajian, editors, *The Rhetoric of the Civil-Rights Movement,* Random House, 1969.

Bracey, John H., Jr., August Meier, and Elliott Rudwick, editors, *Black Nationalism in America,* Bobbs-Merrill, 1970.

Breitman, George, editor, *Malcolm X Speaks: Selected Speeches and Statements,* Pathfinder Press, 1965.

Breitman, George, editor, *By Any Means Necessary: Speeches, Interviews and a Letter by Malcolm X,* Pathfinder Press, 1970.

Clarke, John Henrik, editor, *Malcolm X: The Man and His Times,* Collier, 1969.

Duffy, Bernard K., and Halford R. Ryan, editors, *American Orators of the Twentieth Century: Critical Studies and Sources,* Greenwood Press, 1987.

Dyson, Michael Eric, *Making Malcolm,* Oxford University Press, 1995.

Golden, James L., and Richard D. Rieke, editors, *The Rhetoric of Black Americans,* Charles E. Merrill, 1971.

Goldman, Peter, *The Death and Life of Malcolm X,* Harper, 1973, revised edition, 1979.

Hill, Roy L., editor, *The Rhetoric of Racial Revolt,* Golden Bell Press, 1964.

Holland, DeWitte, editor, *America in Controversy: History of American Public Address,* William C. Brown Company, 1973.

Lincoln, C. Eric, *The Black Muslims in America,* Beacon Press, 1973, revised edition, Kayode Publications, 1991.

Lomax, Louis, *When the Word Is Given...: A Report on Elijah Muhammad, Malcolm X, and the Black Muslim World,* World Publishing, 1963.

Malcolm X (as told to Alex Haley), *The Autobiography of Malcolm X,* Grove, 1965.

Myers, Walter Dean, *Malcolm X: By Any Means Necessary,* Scholastic, 1993.

Perry, Bruce, *Malcolm X: The Last Speeches,* Pathfinder Press, 1989.

Perry, Bruce, *Malcolm: The Life of a Man Who Changed Black America,* Station Hill Press, 1991.

Rummell, Jack, *Malcolm X: Black Militant Leader,* Chelsea House, 1989.

Scott, Robert L., and Wayne Brockriede, *The Rhetoric of Black Power,* Harper, 1969.

Smith, Arthur L., *Rhetoric of Black Revolution,* Allyn & Bacon, 1969.

Smith, Arthur L., and Stephen Robb, editors, *The Voice of Black Rhetoric: Selections,* Allyn & Bacon, 1971.

Periodicals

Detroit Free Press, January 13, 1995; May 2, 1995, p. 5A.

Newsweek, "Back in the Line of Fire," January 23, 1995, pp. 20-22; "A Tale of Two Lonely Lives," January 30, 1995, pp. 46-48; "'I Was in It to Save Lives,'" May 15, 1995, pp. 29-30.

Thurgood Marshall

1908–1993

*Justice of the U.S. Supreme Court and
civil rights activist*

Long before he made history as the first black justice of the U.S. Supreme Court, attorney Thurgood Marshall was known as "Mr. Civil Rights." The nickname honored his lifelong commitment to overturning laws that supported the practice of racial discrimination in the United States. He will forever be linked with one of the greatest legal victories achieved by the National Association for the Advancement of Colored People (NAACP)—the 1954 ruling in Brown v. Board of Education. In this landmark case argued by Marshall when he worked for the NAACP, the U.S. Supreme Court struck down segregation in the nation's public schools. Years later, as the only black on the Supreme Court as well as one of its most liberal members, he worked to preserve and defend hard-won civil rights gains in all areas of American life.

"IN MANY AREAS OF THIS COUNTRY, A WHITE PAROLED MURDERER WOULD BE WELCOME IN PLACES WHICH WOULD AT THE SAME TIME EXCLUDE SUCH PEOPLE AS RALPH BUNCHE, MARIAN ANDERSON, JACKIE ROBINSON, AND MANY OTHERS."

Early Life

Marshall was born in Baltimore, Maryland, and grew up there, except for a five-year period during his infancy and *early childhood when he lived in the Harlem district of New York City. Although he was a good student, he was also known for his fun-loving ways and rebellious spirit. After graduating with honors from Lincoln University in 1929, he tried to enroll in the University of Maryland Law School but was turned down on account of his race. Instead, he attended Howard University Law School.*

Following his graduation (with honors) from Howard in 1933, Marshall went into private practice specializing in civil rights and criminal law. Around the same time, he also began handling some legal work for the local chapter of the NAACP. This led to an invitation in 1936 to become the assistant to the organization's chief counsel (head attorney) at national headquarters in New York City. Two years later, Marshall himself was named chief counsel, and in 1940, he was named head of the newly-created NAACP Legal Defense and Educational Fund.

Leads the NAACP's Court Battles

Under Marshall's leadership, the NAACP came up with a strategy to defeat racial discrimination through the courts by proving that the many restrictive laws then on the books (especially in the South) were unconstitutional. He and his staff worked on a case-by-case basis, challenging unjust treatment experienced by African Americans who tried to vote, make full use of public transportation and public facilities, rent or buy real estate, or serve on a jury or in the armed forces. Marshall personally argued thirty-two cases before the U.S. Supreme Court and won twenty-nine of them.

By far the most famous case he ever took before the Supreme Court was Brown v. Board of Education. *This was actually the collective title of a group of separate lawsuits that all questioned the practice of segregating public school students by race. Supporters of such "separate-but-equal" facilities maintained that the Supreme Court's decision in the* Plessy v. Ferguson *case of 1896 (see box) had guaranteed the right of states to allow segregation in the schools. But Marshall insisted that the "separate-but-equal" policy was unconstitutional because "separate educational facilities are **inherently** unequal."*

inherently: by their very nature.

The Case of *Plessy v. Ferguson*:

One of the most important cases on racial segregation ever to come before the U.S. Supreme Court was *Plessy v. Ferguson* in 1896. The dispute had begun in Louisiana when a black railroad passenger named Homer Plessy was arrested for refusing to leave a whites-only car. He challenged the state law that allowed such segregation, but a judge in Louisiana ruled against him.

Plessy then appealed to the U.S. Supreme Court, which also upheld the Louisiana law ordering separate railroad cars for whites and blacks. The Supreme Court justices based their decision on their interpretation of the Fourteenth Amendment to the Constitution. They agreed that this amendment had guaranteed political equality for blacks. But they did not think that it meant to guarantee *social* equality, which they said would lead to "a mixing of the two races upon terms unsatisfactory to either." In short, concluded the justices, having separate railroad cars for whites and blacks was "reasonable" as long as the accommodations for blacks were "equal" to those for whites.

By issuing such a decision, the Supreme Court officially approved the idea of legal racial segregation. This made it possible for "separate-but-equal" public facilities for blacks to exist in the United States—mostly across the South—for more than fifty years.

*On May 17, 1954, the U.S. Supreme Court decided in favor of Marshall and the NAACP, ruling **unanimously** that the segregation of black and white students in the public schools was indeed unconstitutional. Earlier that spring, when it appeared that victory might be near, an upbeat Marshall addressed an audience at Dillard University in New Orleans, Louisiana. In his speech, he discussed the great strides that had been made toward achieving integration in the United States. He also touched on what still remained to be done. A brief excerpt from his long lecture follows. It is reprinted here from* The Voice of Black America: Major Speeches by Negroes in the United States, 1797–1971, *edited by Philip S. Foner, Simon & Schuster, 1972.*

❝

There has been much discussion during recent years concerning the question of the removal in this country of dual citizenship based solely on race and color. The primary emphasis has been on the elimination of

unanimously: with the agreement or consent of everyone.

racial segregation. No one denies that progress is being made. There are, however, some who say that the progress is too slow and others who say that the progress is too rapid. The important thing to remember is that progress is being made.... We are moving toward a completely integrated society, North and South.

Those who doubt this and those who are afraid of complete integration are victims of a background based upon long **indoctrination** of only one side of the controversy in this country.... They know only of one side of slavery. They know only the biased reports about Reconstruction and the long-standing theory which seems to support the "legality" of the separate-but-equal doctrine....

Our government is based on the principle of the equality of man the individual, not the group.... Our basic legal document, the Constitution of the United States, guarantees equal protection of the laws to all of us. Many state constitutions have similar provisions.... These high-sounding principles we preach and teach. However, in the eyes of the world we stand convicted of violating these principles day in and day out.

Today ... we have a society where, in varying degrees throughout the country, but especially in the South, Negroes, solely because they are Negroes, are segregated, **ostracized** and set apart from all other Americans. This discrimination extends from the cradle to the graveyard.... Or, to put it even more bluntly, in many areas of this country, a white paroled murderer would be welcome in places which would at the same time exclude such people as [Nobel Prize winner] **Ralph Bunche** [see entry], [singer] Marian Anderson, [baseball star] Jackie Robinson, and many others. Constitutionally protected individual rights have been effectively destroyed by **outmoded** theories of racial or group inferiority. Why is this true? How long can we afford the luxury of segregation and discrimination?

One reason this condition of dual citizenship exists is because we have been conditioned to an acceptance of this theory [of racial inequality] as a fact. We are the products of a misunderstanding of history....

Our society is the victim of the following periods of history: the period of slavery, when the slaveholders defended slavery by repeating over and over again the myth that slavery

indoctrination: education intended to influence someone to think or feel a certain way.

ostracized: excluded, shut out.

outmoded: old-fashioned, obsolete.

An all-black segregated school before Brown v. Board of Education

was not only a positive good for the nation but was absolutely beneficial and necessary for the Negroes themselves. Consequently, even free Negroes were denied the right of citizenship and subjected to all manner of abuse without legal **redress.** Immediately following the Civil War, and indeed up to the 1930s, is the period when Negroes were no longer slaves but were certainly not yet full citizens. Having passed through this **laissez-faire** period in so far as **asserting** our Constitutional rights is concerned, Negroes began in the thirties the all-out fight to secure the right to vote and at the same time to break down discrimination and segregation....

In so far as securing the right to vote ... much progress has been made to the end that as of the 1948 national elections, at least 1,300,000 Negroes voted in the deep South....

redress: compensation, a way of righting a wrong done to someone.

laissez-faire: a belief, usually in economics, that the government should make as few regulations as possible.

asserting: claiming.

Thurgood Marshall

In the North we have seen the drive for protection of the right to work without regard to race and color....

We have also seen the breaking-down of the legal barriers to owning and occupying real property without regard to race or color....

As of the present time, the **paramount** issue in so far as Americanism is concerned is the ending of all racial distinctions in American life. The reasons for this are many. A weighty factor, of course, is the recognition by more and more people in high places that the world situation in regard to the sensitive areas throughout the world depends on how well we can handle our race problem in this country....

Racial segregation in our country is immoral, costly, and damaging to the nation's prestige....

We have to ask whether or not ... our country can afford to continue in practicing *not* what they preach.... All of us know that segregation traditionally results in unequal facilities for the segregated group. Duplication of facilities is expensive, **diverts** funds from the economy which could be utilized to improve facilities for all groups. Finally, segregation leads to the blockage of real communication between the two groups. In turn, this blockage increases **mutual** suspicion, distrust, hostility, stereotypes and prejudice; and these, all together, result in a social climate of tension favorable to aggressive behavior and social disorganization which sometimes **culminate** in race riots....

Everyone in and out of government must understand that the future of our government and indeed the world depends on the recognition of the equality of man—the principle which is inherent in the theory of our government and protected by our Constitution.

Of course, we have made progress, but instead of gloating over this progress, we should get renewed courage to tackle the next job....

There are still those who will continue to tell us that law is one thing and **ethics** another. However, I prefer to follow what one legal historian has stated—"Laws and ethics, some men bluntly tell us are separate fields. So indeed they are. But

paramount: dominant, most important.

diverts: shifts in another direction.

mutual: shared.

culminate: result.

ethics: the set of moral principles or values that influence individual or group behavior.

Thurgood Marshall

spare America the day when both together do not determine the meaning of equal protection of the laws."

We must understand the slavery background of segregation and we must understand the complete lack of any scientific support for racial superiority or inferiority. We must understand that racial segregation is violative of every religious principle.... We must never forget what racial segregation did to our parents and is doing to us, and how it will affect our children. We must turn from misunderstanding and fear to intelligent planning, courage and determination....

The results of an effort to get a full picture of desegregation in American communities are now available. And it is hoped that these results can be passed on to every American

Marshall, Chief Counsel for NAACP, at Supreme Court Building, 1958

and to our friends and critics overseas. For these results clearly show that in the past ten years, America has undergone a startling, dramatic and completely **unprecedented** change in race relations—and all for the better. Racial desegregation has been attempted successfully in literally hundreds of instances, in all regions, and in all walks of life. In addition to the more noticeable areas of schools and the armed forces, complete success has been reported in desegregating public-housing projects, labor unions, Catholic and Protestant churches, public and private swimming pools, professional organizations, some YMCAs and many YWCAs, Southern industries, ...officers' and enlisted men's clubs and housing areas on Army posts, hospitals, summer camps, and many other areas—even cemeteries.

An impressive part of these great changes is the way that the "unthinkables" of ten years ago have become the "taken-for-granteds" of today....

Why have people decided to desegregate? Members of American communities have tried to integrate their institutions for an extremely varied number of reasons. The pressures to desegregate have come from several forces—sometimes from an aroused Negro community, sometimes from administrative rulings of local authorities, sometimes from rulings by a national body, sometimes from voluntary decision by a majority of concerned community members....

The accomplishment of effective and efficient desegregation with a minimum of social disturbance depends on the following five things:

1. There must be a clear and **unequivocal** statement of policy by leaders with prestige, and by authority officials.

2. There must be firm enforcement and persistent execution of the nonsegregation policy in the face of initial resistance.

3. Authorities and law enforcement officials must show a willingness to deal with violations, attempted violations or **incitement** to violations, by applying the law and backing it up with strong enforcement action.

unprecedented: never before seen or experienced.

unequivocal: definite, without any doubt whatsoever.

incitement: encouragement.

Thurgood Marshall

4. Authorities must refuse to employ, engage in or tolerate **subterfuges, gerrymandering** or other devices for evading the principle and the fact of desegregation.

5. The accomplishment of desegregation must be accompanied by continual interpretation of the reasons for the action, and appealing to the democratic and moral values of all persons involved.

In conclusion, racial segregation is grounded upon the myth of inherent racial superiority. This myth has been completely exploded by all scientific studies. It now stands exposed as a theory which can only be explained as a **vehicle** for **perpetuating** racial prejudice. History reveals that racial segregation is a badge of slavery, is just as unscientifically supported, immoral and un-American as slavery. Recent history shows that it can be removed, and that it can be done effectively when approached intelligently.

There is no longer any justification for segregation. There is no longer any excuse for it. There is no longer any reason under the sun why intelligent people should continue to find excuses for not ending segregation in their own community, in the South as well as in the North.

99

*Marshall's career took a different turn in 1961, when President John F. Kennedy nominated him to a federal judgeship on the U.S. Court of Appeals. Southern segregationists who were fiercely opposed to appointing an African American to the post held up the **confirmation** process for nearly a year. But in the end, Marshall was confirmed.*

In 1965, President Lyndon Johnson named Marshall solicitor general. In this position, he argued cases before the U.S. Supreme Court on behalf of the federal government. Two years later, the president again turned to Marshall, this time to fill a vacancy on the U.S. Supreme Court. As before, a group of Southern congressmen opposed to his race, his liberal views, and his activist past tried to prevent him from being confirmed. But they quickly met with

subterfuges: tricks.

gerrymandering: dividing an area (such as a voting district) in such a way that a certain group has advantages over other groups.

vehicle: means or way.

perpetuating: causing to continue.

confirmation: approval.

defeat, and Marshall went on to make history as the first African American to serve on the nation's highest court.

During the more than twenty years he served as an associate justice, Marshall stood firm against a rising tide of **conservatism** *that influenced many of the Supreme Court's rulings throughout the 1970s and 1980s. All of his decisions reflected his firm belief that the rights of the individual are always more important than the rights of the state.*

In 1990, Marshall retired from the Supreme Court. He told reporters that his advancing age and failing health had made him decide to step down. But some people guessed that perhaps he had just grown tired of battling his opponents on the Court. He died of heart failure on January 24, 1993.

Sources

Books

Aldred, Lisa, *Thurgood Marshall,* Chelsea House, 1990.

Baird, A. Craig, editor, *Representative American Speeches: 1953–1954,* Wilson, 1954.

Broderick, Francis L., and August Meier, editors, *Negro Protest Thought in the Twentieth Century,* Bobbs-Merrill, 1965.

Davis, Michael D., and Hunter R. Clark, *Thurgood Marshall: Warrior at the Bar, Rebel on the Bench,* Carol Publishing, 1992.

Foner, Philip S., editor, *The Voice of Black America: Major Speeches by Negroes in the United States, 1797–1971,* Simon & Schuster, 1972.

Golden, James L., and Richard D. Rieke, *The Rhetoric of Black Americans,* Charles E. Merrill, 1971.

Goldman, Roger, and David Gallen, *Thurgood Marshall: Justice for All,* Carroll & Graf, 1992.

Grunewald, Donald, editor, *"I Am Honored to Be Here Today...": Commencement Speeches by Notable Personalities,* Oceana Publications, 1985.

Rowan, Carl T., *Dream Makers, Dream Breakers: The World of Thurgood Marshall,* Little, Brown, 1992.

conservatism: a political philosophy that favors moderation and that is inclined to follow tradition and reject or be suspicious of change.

Williams, Jamye Coleman, and McDonald Williams, editors, *The Negro Speaks: The Rhetoric of Contemporary Black Leaders,* Noble & Noble, 1970.

Periodicals

Ebony, "The Thurgood Marshall Nobody Knows," May 1990, pp. 68-76; "Forty-Five Years in Law and Civil Rights," November 1990, pp. 80-86.

Newsweek, "A Great Original's Lives at the Law: Thurgood Marshall Made as Much History in Front of the Supreme Court as He Did Serving It," July 8, 1991.

People, "Justices Marshall and Brennan Battle to Keep Liberalism Alive at the U.S. Supreme Court," July 7, 1986, pp. 53-54; "A Warrior Retires: The Son of a Black Steward in an All-White Club Rewrote the Rules about Race," July 15, 1991.

Time, "Negro Justice," June 23, 1967, pp. 18-19; "The First Negro Justice," September 8, 1967, p. 16; "A Lawyer Who Changed America," July 8, 1991.

U.S. News and World Report, "With Mr. Marshall on the Supreme Court," June 26, 1967, pp. 12-13; "With Another 'Liberal' on High Court," September 11, 1967, p. 21; "Embracing a Great Man's Gift to America," July 8, 1991.

Carol Moseley-Braun

1947–

Member of the U.S. Senate

"THE EMBLEMS OF THE CONFEDERACY HAVE MEANING TO AMERICANS EVEN ONE HUNDRED YEARS AFTER THE END OF THE CIVIL WAR. WHEN WE SEE THE CONFEDERATE SYMBOLS HAULED OUT, EVERYBODY KNOWS WHAT THAT MEANS."

In November 1992, Carol Moseley-Braun made history when she became the first black woman (and the first black Democrat) to be elected to the United States Senate. Her victory in the Illinois race came in a year that saw many voters express their disgust with "politics-as-usual." They did so by supporting a record number of female and minority candidates for office at the local, state, and national level. But none of those campaigns generated as much interest as that of Moseley-Braun and her startling rise to fame. She had not even been expected to survive the primary election, let alone triumph in the general election.

Early Life and Career

The daughter of a police officer and a medical technician, Moseley-Braun was born and raised in Chicago, Illinois. She received her bachelor's degree (1967) and her law degree (1972) from the University of Chicago. Her first try at elective office came in 1978 when she ran for the Illinois state legislature. She beat eleven other candidates despite her lack of political experience. Four years later, Moseley-Braun became the first woman to serve as assistant majority leader. She also acted as Chicago Mayor Harold Washington's official spokesperson in the legislature. In 1987, a year after losing out in a bid to become her party's nominee for lieutenant governor, Moseley-Braun ran for the position of Cook County recorder of deeds. In a county dominated by Democrats, she easily defeated her Republican opponent.

*Moseley-Braun's decision to enter national politics took shape during the fall of 1991. Like so many other Americans, she watched with great interest that October as the all-male, all-white Senate Judiciary Committee held confirmation hearings for Supreme Court hopeful **Clarence Thomas** (see entry). Appearing before the committee was Anita Hill, a University of Oklahoma law professor and former government employee. Hill, a black woman, claimed that Thomas (who was also black) had sexually harassed her at work years earlier. Despite her charges and the public outcry that followed, Thomas was eventually confirmed as a Supreme Court justice. Among those who voted for him was Illinois Senator Alan Dixon.*

Convinced by what she had seen and heard that government officials had "lost touch" with the people, Moseley-Braun made up her mind to challenge Dixon for his Senate seat in the March 1992 primary election. She faced tremendous odds—Dixon had a great deal of money available for his campaign, and he had never before been defeated in his forty-year-long political career. Nevertheless, Moseley-Braun pulled off a stunning upset over Dixon and millionaire lawyer Albert Hofeld. Both men had ferociously battled each other while virtually ignoring their low-key opponent.

This unexpected victory made Moseley-Braun an overnight star on the national political scene. All signs indicated she was destined to capture the historic national senate seat in the upcoming general election. But her rather casual and disorganized campaign nearly fell apart in its final weeks due to rumors of staff problems and hints that she had not handled all of her personal financial affairs in a completely honest manner. On election day, she experienced

victory over Republican Richard Williamson, a wealthy lawyer from suburban Chicago who had served as a senior aide in the administration of President Ronald Reagan.

Heads to Washington, D.C.

Moseley-Braun's first few months as a U.S. senator were somewhat rocky. She was often distracted by controversies about her campaign and her personal life and criticism of her conduct and judgment. Eventually, though, Moseley-Braun settled into her new role. She accepted three committee assignments, including one on the Senate Judiciary Committee (the same committee whose actions during the Clarence Thomas hearings had first inspired her to run for national office). Early on in her term, she also established herself as a highly visible advocate of various liberal causes.

At no time were Moseley-Braun's beliefs more clear than on July 22, 1993, when she experienced a truly great moment in her political career. During the course of business that day, Jesse Helms, the Republican senator from North Carolina, proposed an amendment to a piece of legislation known as the National and Community Service Act. His amendment would have granted a congressional design patent—an honorary stamp of approval—to the emblem of the United Daughters of the Confederacy. (UDC members are descendants of men who fought for the South during the Civil War.) As outlined in the amendment, the UDC emblem featured the original Confederate flag encircled by a wreath.

To Moseley-Braun, the congressional patent for the UDC emblem was an unacceptable and offensive tribute to slavery and racism. After South Carolina Senator Strom Thurmond spoke up in support of Helms's amendment, Moseley-Braun asked for the opportunity to respond. In a voice that often shook with emotion, she passionately argued against giving official Senate recognition to such a painful symbol of the past. Her words are taken from the Congressional Record, *103rd Congress, 1st session, July 22, 1993, pp. S9252-S9270.*

❝

Mr. President [Senator Bob Kerry, the Presiding Officer of the Senate], I would like to respond to this amendment and to suggest that it is absolutely ill-founded....

I think it is important to note what a design patent is. It is not just a matter of simple recognition. It is a rare honor given to an organization. There are very few of them given....

I submit further that the design patent is not needed in terms of the work of the organization. The Senator from South Carolina has gone on at great length to talk about the charitable work of the United Daughters of the Confederacy. The fact of the matter is the refusal to extend this extraordinary honor by this body does not stop them from doing whatever it is they do, from continuing their work in the community and the like.... The only issue is whether or not this body is prepared to put its **imprimatur** on the Confederate insignia used by the United Daughters of the Confederacy.

I submit to you, Mr. President, and the members who are listening to this debate ... that the United Daughters of the Confederacy have every right to honor their ancestors and to choose the Confederate flag as their symbol if they like. However, those of us whose ancestors fought on a different side in the Civil War, or who were held, frankly, as human chattel under the Confederate flag, are duty bound to honor our ancestors as well by asking whether such recognition by the U.S. Senate is appropriate....

I have heard the argument on the floor today with regard to the imprimatur that is being sought for this organization and for this symbol, and I submit this really is **revisionist history.** The fact of the matter is the emblems of the Confederacy have meaning to Americans even one hundred years after the end of the Civil War. Everybody knows what the Confederacy stands for. Everybody knows what the insignia means. That matter of common knowledge is not a surprise to any of us. When a former governor [George Wallace] stood and raised the Confederate battle flag over the Alabama State Capitol to protest the federal government support for civil rights and a visit by the attorney general at the time in 1963, everybody knew what that meant. Now, in this time, in 1993, when we see the Confederate symbols hauled out, everybody knows what that means.

So I submit, as Americans we have an obligation, Number 1, to recognize the meaning, not to fall prey to revisionist history on the one hand; and also really to make a statement that we believe the Civil War is over. We believe that as Americans we are all Americans and have a need to be respectful of one another with regard to our respective histories....

imprimatur: a mark of official approval.

revisionist history: a way of interpreting the past in a new way, usually with a specific idea or system of beliefs in mind.

Carol Moseley-Braun

Whether we are black or white, northerners or southerners, all Americans share a common history, and we share a common flag. The flag which is behind you right now, Mr. President, is our flag. The flag, the Stars and Stripes forever, is our flag, whether we are from the North or South, whether we are African Americans or not—that is our flag. And to give a design patent that even our own flag does not enjoy to a symbol of the confederacy seems to be just to create the kind of divisions in our society that are counterproductive, that are not needed.

So I come back to the point I raised to begin with. What is the point of doing this? Why would we give an extraordinary honor to a symbol which is counter to the symbol that we as Americans, I believe, all know and love, which would be a recognition of the losing side of the war, a war that I hope— while it is a painful part of our history—I hope as Americans we have all gotten past and we can say as Americans we come together under a single flag? And this organization, if it chooses to honor the losing side of the Civil War, that is their **prerogative.** But it is inappropriate for that organization to call on the rest of us, on everybody else, to give our imprimatur to the symbolism of the Confederate flag.

Symbols are important. They speak volumes to the people in our country. They speak volumes to the people outside of our country who follow and who care about what happens in this, the greatest nation in the world. It seems to me the time has long passed when we could put behind us the debates and arguments that have raged since the Civil War, that we get beyond the separateness and we get beyond the divisions and we get beyond fanning the flames of racial **antagonism.** I submit that to use the insignia of the United Daughters is their prerogative. However, it is not their prerogative to force me and other members of this body to **assent** to an extraordinary honor of their own revisionist history. That is the purpose of the design patent.

[A few minutes later, the Senate voted on a motion to reject the amendment. Forty-eight senators were in favor of doing so, but fifty-two were not. An angry Moseley-Braun once again asked to be heard.]

Madam President [Senator Barbara Boxer, the Presiding Officer of the Senate], I really had not wanted

prerogative: right, choice.
antagonism: hatred.
assent: agree, approve.

to have to do this because in my remarks I believe that I was restrained and tempered.... I talked about how it was not necessary for this organization to receive the design patent extension, which was an extraordinary extension of an extraordinary act to begin with. What I did not talk about and what I am **constrained** now to talk about with no small degree of emotion is the symbolism of what this vote—

[Moseley-Braun was at this point interrupted by the presiding officer, who called the Senate to order.]

That is what this vote really means.

I started off—maybe—I do not know—it is just my day to get to talk about race. Maybe I am just lucky about that today.

I have to tell you this vote is about race. It is about racial symbolism. It is about racial symbols, the racial past, and the single most painful episode in American history....

I am really stunned by how often and how much the issue of race, the subject of racism, comes up in this U.S. Senate, comes up in this body and how I have to, on many occasions, as the only African American here, constrain myself to be calm, to be laid back, to talk about these issues in very intellectual, nonemotional terms, and that is what I do on a regular basis, Madam President. That is part and parcel of my daily existence.

But at the same time, when the issue of the design patent extension for the United Daughters of the Confederacy first came up, I looked at it. I did not make a big deal of it. It came as part of the work of the Judiciary Committee. I looked at it, and I said, well, I am not going to vote for that.

When I announced that I was not going to vote for it, the chairman, as was his due, began to poll the members. We talked about it, and I found myself getting drawn into a debate that I frankly never expected.

Who would have expected a design patent for the Confederate flag? And there are those in this body who say this really is not the Confederate flag. The other thing we did know was a Confederate flag.

constrained: obliged, forced.

I did my research, and I looked it up as I am wont to do, and guess what? That is the real Confederate flag. The thing we see all the time and are accustomed to is the battle flag....

This flag is the real flag of the Confederacy. If there is anybody in this chamber, anybody, indeed anybody in this world, that has a doubt that the Confederate effort was around preserving the institution of slavery, I am prepared and I believe history is prepared to dispute them.... There is no question but that battle was fought to try to preserve our nation, to keep the states from separating themselves over the issue of whether or not my ancestors could be held as property, as chattel, as objects of commerce and trade in this country.

And people died. More Americans died in the Civil War than any war they have ever gone through since. People died

Moseley-Braun at microphone: "I am going to call it like I see it, as I always do."

over the proposition that indeed these United States stood for the proposition that every person was created equal without regard to race, that we are all American citizens.

I am sorry, Madam President. I will lower my voice. I am getting excited, because, quite frankly, that is the very issue. The issue is whether or not Americans, such as myself, who believe in the promise of this country, who feel strongly and who are patriots in this country, will have to suffer the indignity of being reminded time and time again, that at one point in this country's history we were human chattel. We were property. We could be traded, bought, and sold.

Now, to suggest as a matter of revisionist history that this flag is not about slavery flies in the face of history, Madam President.

I was not going to get **inflammatory.** In fact, my staff brought me this little thing earlier, and it has been sitting here. I do not know if you noticed it sitting here during the earlier debate in which I was **dispassionate** and tried my level best not to be emotional … and not get into calling names and talking about race and racism. I did not use it to begin with. I do want to share it now. It is a speech by the Vice President of the Confederate States of America, March 21, 1861, in Savannah, Georgia.

"Slavery, the Cornerstone of the Confederacy," and this man goes on to say:

> The new Confederate constitution has put to rest forever all agitating questions relating to our peculiar "institution," which is what they called it. African slavery as it exists among us, the proper status of a Negro in our form of civilization. This was the immediate cause of the late rupture and present revolution.

> The prevailing ideas entertained by Thomas Jefferson and most of the leading statesmen at the time of the formation of the old Constitution were that the enslavement of the African was in violation of the laws of nature, that it was wrong in principle, socially, morally, and politically.

And then he goes on to say:

> Our new government is founded upon exactly the opposite idea. Its foundations are laid, its cornerstone rests upon the

inflammatory: intended to spark anger, provocative.

dispassionate: calm, unemotional.

Carol Moseley-Braun

great truth that the Negro is not equal to the white man, that slavery, subordination to the superior race is his natural and moral condition.

This was a statement by the Vice President of the Confederate States of America.

Madam President, across the room on the other side is the flag. I say to you it is outrageous. It is an absolute outrage that this body would adopt as an amendment to this legislation a symbol of this point of view and, Madam President, I say to you that it is an important issue. It is a symbolic issue up there. There is no way you can get around it.

The reason for my emotion—I have been here almost seven months now, and my colleagues will tell you there is not a more congenial, laid back, even person in this entire body who makes it a point to try to get along with everybody. I make it a point to try to talk to my colleagues and get beyond controversy and conflict, to try to find consensus on issues.

But I say to you, Madam President, on this issue there can be no consensus. It is an outrage. It is an insult. It is absolutely unacceptable to me and to millions of Americans, black or white, that we would put the imprimatur of the United States Senate on a symbol of this kind of idea. And that is what is at stake with this amendment, Madam President.

I am going to continue—I am going to continue because I am going to call it like I see it, as I always do. I was appalled, appalled at a segment of my own Democratic Party that would go take a walk and vote for something like this.

I am going to talk for a minute first about my brethren, my close-in brethren, and then talk about the other side of the aisle and the responsibility of the Republican Party.

The reason the Republican Party got run out on a rail the last time is the American people sensed intolerance in that party. The American people, African Americans sensed there was not room for them in that party. Folks took a look at the convention and said, my God, what are these people standing for? This is not America. And they turned around and voted for change. They elected Bill Clinton president and the rest of us to this chamber. The changes they were speaking out for was a change that said we have to get past racism, we have to get past sexism, the many issues that divide us as Americans, and come together as Americans so we can make this country be what it can be in the twenty-first century.

That is the real reason, Madam President, that I am here today. My state has less than twelve percent African Americans in it, but the people of Illinois had no problem voting for a candidate that was African American because they thought they were doing the same thing.

Similarly, the state of California sent two women, two women to the U.S. Senate, breaking a gender barrier, as did the state of Washington. Why? Because they felt it was time to get past the barriers that said that women had no place in the conduct of our business.

And so, just as our country is moving forward, Madam President, to have this kind of symbol shoved in your face, shoved in my face, shoved in the faces of all the Americans who want to see a change for us to get beyond racism, is singularly inappropriate.

I say to you, Madam President, that this is no small matter. This is not a matter of little old ladies walking around doing good deeds. There is no reason why these little old ladies cannot do good deeds anyway. If they choose to wave the Confederate flag, that certainly is their right. Because I care about the fact that this is a free country. Free speech is the cornerstone of democracy. People are supposed to be able to say what they want to say. They are supposed to be able to join associations and organizations that express their views.

But I daresay, Madam President, that following the Civil War, and following the victory of the United States and the coming together of our country, that that peculiar institution was put to rest for once and for all; that the division in our nation, the North versus the South, was put to rest once and for all. And the people of this country do not want to see a day in which flags like that are underwritten, underscored, adopted, approved by this U.S. Senate.

That is what this vote is about. That is what this vote is about.

Carol Moseley-Braun

I say to you, Madam President, I do not know—I do not want to yield the floor right now because I do not know what will happen next.

I will yield momentarily to my colleague from California, Madam President, because I think that this is an issue that I am not going—if I have to stand here until this room freezes over, I am not going to see this amendment put on this legislation which has to do with national service.

[After the presiding officer confirmed that Moseley-Braun had agreed to give up the floor briefly to allow someone else to speak, the senator from Illinois concluded her remarks.]

If I have to stand here until this room freezes over, Madam President, I am going to do so. Because I will tell you, this is something that has no place in this body. It has no place in the Senate. It has no place in our society.

And the fact is, Madam President, that I would encourage my colleagues on both sides of the aisle—Republican and Democrat; those who thought, "Well, we are just going to do this, you know, because it is no big deal"—to understand what a very big deal indeed it is—that the imprimatur that is being sought here today sends a sign out to the rest of this country that that peculiar institution has not been put to bed for once and for all; that, indeed, like Dracula, it has come back to haunt us time and time and time again; and that, in spite of the fact that we have made strides forward, the fact of the matter is that there are those who would keep us slipping back into the darkness of division, into the snake pit of racial hatred, of racial antagonism and of support for symbols—symbols of the struggle to keep African Americans, Americans of African descent, in bondage.

[After some more debate, another vote was taken on the motion to drop the amendment. This time, seventy-five senators voted yes, and twenty-five voted no. An emotional Moseley-Braun thanked her colleagues "for having the heart, having the intellect, having the mind and the will to turn around what, in my mind, would have been a tragic mistake." She ended her remarks with the observation that follows.]

As a student of history and mathematics, I have said this to people before. There is something called factor addition in mathematics that says you add forces working together, you subtract forces working against each other, and that, Madam President, is the message and the lesson of things like what happened here today, the lesson that if we work together as Americans, we will be the great country that this Constitution defines and our Declaration of Independence set out and that so many people hold so dear in their heart. We will be able to give pride and real meaning to that flag, the flag of the United States, that is the flag that we all love because we love this country and because we know that in its diversity is its strength.

Moseley-Braun's electrifying performance in this debate has been overshadowed by her continuing financial problems. Federal investigators have been looking into her 1992 campaign expenses, and she may eventually face fines for improper spending and sloppy record-keeping. In addition, she is still more than $500,000 in debt from that same campaign.

Raising money to wipe out that debt and prepare for a re-election campaign in 1998 has been one of Braun's biggest challenges. Many of her old followers feel she has abandoned her liberal principles because she has voted with the Republicans in favor of bills that help big businesses. And a number of African Americans in Illinois were disturbed by the fact that she so warmly supported Chicago Mayor Richard M. Daley, a white man, in his 1995 re-election bid. His opponents in that race were two black progressives who had backed Moseley-Braun during her run for the Senate.

Mosely-Braun pointed out that she has remained true to the liberal position by battling against the Republicans on issues such as affirmative action (programs designed to remedy the effects of past discrimination in jobs and schools and to end such discrimination), the environment, and welfare. Her support for business, she said, is driven by her belief that companies must stay healthy and profitable to create more jobs. As Moseley-Braun put it, "I'm forging a position in the moral center of the debates here in Washington."

Sources

Periodicals

Congressional Record, 103rd Congress, 1st session, July 22, 1993, pp. S9252-S9270.

Jet, "Carol Moseley-Braun Makes Victorious Stand in Senate Against Confederate Flag," August 9, 1993, pp. 4-6.

Newsweek, "The Trials and Troubles of a Symbolic Senator," April 8, 1996, pp. 34-35.

Time, "Nixing Dixie," August 2, 1993, p. 30.

Adam Clayton Powell, Jr.

1908–1972
Politician and minister

Adam Clayton Powell, Jr., was a colorful and controversial figure on the American political scene for nearly thirty years. The mention of his name still provokes widely different reactions. To some people, he was a hard-working civil rights advocate who courageously challenged the status quo (the existing state of affairs). To others, he was an immoral playboy and deal-maker with a talent for self-promotion. In truth, Powell was a little of both.

Early Life

Powell was born in New Haven, Connecticut, but grew up in New York City's Harlem district. There his father, Adam Sr., served as pastor of the well-known and highly respected Abyssinian Baptist Church. (In addition to being the oldest black congregation in the North, Abyssinian Baptist was also at that time one of the largest Protestant congregations in the entire United States.) Adam Jr. went on to earn his undergraduate degree from Colgate University in

1930 and his master's degree from Columbia University in 1932. He then returned to Abyssinian Baptist as an assistant. In 1936, he took over as pastor when his father retired from preaching. Two years later, he received his Doctor of Divinity degree from Shaw University.

From the very beginning, the scrappy and sharp-tongued Powell combined his ministry with community activism. As a result, he quickly earned a reputation as a fearless rabble-rouser (someone who stirs up a crowd). One of his biggest and most successful efforts forced big businesses and government offices that operated in Harlem to hire more blacks. To bring about this change, he organized and led picket lines, boycotts, strikes, and other demonstrations. Powell also developed a number of social and welfare programs at his church. Among them were a vocational guidance clinic, a soup kitchen, and a distribution center that provided food, clothing, and heating fuel to Harlem's poorest residents.

A Move to Politics

In 1941, Powell was elected to the New York City Council. Three years later, after voting districts were redrawn, he became the first person to hold the newly-created seat in the U.S. House of Representatives that included Harlem. Once in Washington, D.C., he continued his fight against racial injustice. He vowed that his only goal was to obtain the total integration of blacks into the political and economic structure of the United States.

Wherever he went, Powell created shock waves. He boldly defied the many unwritten rules barring him from certain public places such as dining rooms and barber shops. Time and time again on the House floor, he furiously challenged Southern segregationists who tried to block civil rights legislation. He also denounced racism in public transportation and introduced a bill that would have denied federal funds to projects that tolerated discrimination.

From 1960 until 1967, Powell served as chairman of the House Committee on Education and Labor. This prestigious position made him one of the most powerful African Americans in the country. During his time in office, the committee

Adam Clayton Powell, Jr.

passed nearly fifty significant pieces of social legislation dealing with such issues as the minimum wage, juvenile delinquency, and vocational education.

Criticized for Behavior and Beliefs

Not surprisingly, Powell's confrontational style led to problems. He clashed with his colleagues in both political parties and with other government officials, including the president. He also quarreled with labor leaders and educators.

As the years went by, Powell's personal lifestyle began to raise quite a few eyebrows. He was often seen in the company of beautiful female "associates" while wearing expensive clothes, driving luxury cars, and jetting off on long *vacations. This angered many people who felt he was not taking his job seriously. Others wondered if he was perhaps mismanaging the money that he was supposed to use to run his office. Powell responded to these concerns with his typical bluntness, declaring that he was only doing "right out in the open" all of the "things other congressmen try to hide."*

During the early 1960s, Powell irritated a number of people both inside and outside the government with his outspoken support of the black power movement. His views contrasted sharply with that of mainstream civil rights leaders, who had been cool—if not downright hostile—to the black power philosophy. But time and time again, Powell publicly thumbed his nose at those he referred to as "ceremonial Negro leaders."

One especially memorable occasion was on May 29, 1966, when he was a guest at Howard University in Washington, D.C. At graduation ceremonies that day, Powell delivered what is considered to be his most famous speech on the subject of black power. A flery orator who could hold an audience spellbound, he was deliberately provocative and dramatic in this and in most of his other speeches. Excerpts from his remarks are reprinted here primarily from Rhetoric of Black Revolution, *by Arthur L. Smith, Allyn & Bacon, 1969, with some additional text from* The Voice of Black America: Major Speeches by Negroes in the United States, 1797–1971, *edited by Philip S. Foner, Simon & Schuster, 1972.*

66

Can there any good thing come out of Nazareth?

Almost two thousand years ago, that question was a **contemptuous** inquiry in the book of John [in the Bible].

"And Nathanael said unto Philip, 'Can there any good thing come out of Nazareth?' Philip saith, 'Come and see.'" Nazareth was the Mississippi of Galilee. There were no great artists or philosopher-kings or musicians. There was no center of learning such as Howard University. In this commence-

contemptuous: scornful; lacking respect.

ment of your life, the world will ask: Can there any good thing come out of Howard?

As black students educated at America's finest black institution of higher learning, you are still second-class citizens. A mere one hundred years in the spectrum of time separates us from the history of slavery and a lifetime of indignities. Next year, on March 2, 1967, Howard will celebrate the centennial of its founding. Next year, on March 21, 1967, the Committee on Education and Labor of which I am the chairman will also celebrate its one-hundredth anniversary.

How ironic that the Committee on Education and Labor which was formed immediately after the Civil War to help black slaves make the transition into freedom should have a black man one hundred years later as its chairman.... While both Howard and I as chairman of this committee will celebrate our one hundred years together, joy of our success is tempered by the sobering fact that our status as black people has been denied first-class acceptance....

To possess a black skin today in America means that if you are in Los Angeles driving your pregnant wife to a hospital, you'll be shot to death by a white policeman.

A black skin means that if your family lives in Webster County, Mississippi, your average family income will be $846 a year—$16.30 a week for an entire family.

A black skin today is an unemployment rate twice that of whites, despite a skyrocketing gross national product ... and an unprecedented level of employment.

A black skin means you are still a child, that all the white liberals who have helped you to take your first steps toward freedom and manhood now believe they own your soul, can manage your lives and control your civil rights organizations....

So beware not only of Greeks bearing gifts, but colored men seeking loans and Northern white liberals!

At this graduation today, this is the reality of self you must face. Your graduation comes at a particularly critical period of the black man's searching **reassessment** of who he is, what he should become and how he should become IT. The history of the last twenty-five years of the freedom struggle has been **capsuled** in only two concepts: integration and civil rights.

reassessment: new or revised judgment of something's importance or value.

capsuled: condensed into.

Adam Clayton Powell, Jr.

During those years, our leaders—and black people are the only people who have "leaders"; other groups have politicians, statesmen, educators, financiers and businessmen—but during those years, our leaders drugged us with the LSD of integration. Instead of telling us to seek **audacious** power—more black power—instead of leading us in the pursuit of excellence, our leaders led us in the sterile chase of integration as an end in itself in the **debasing** notion that a few white skins sprinkled amongst us would somehow elevate the genetics of our development.

As a result, ours was an integration of intellectual **mediocrity,** economic inferiority and political **subservience.** Like frightened children, we were afraid to eat the strong meat of human rights and instead sucked the milk of civil rights from the breasts of white liberals, black Uncle Toms and Aunt Jemimas....

Historically, strong meat was too risky for most black people for it would have enabled them to **discern** both good and evil, the difference between civil rights and human rights.

Human rights are God-given. Civil rights are manmade. Civil rights has been that grand deception practiced by those who have not placed God first, who have not believed that God-given rights can empower the black man with superiority as well as equality.

Our life must be purposed to **implement** human rights:

- The right to be secure in one's person from the excessive abuses of the state and its law-enforcing officials.

- The right to freedom of choice of a job to feed one's family.

- The right to freedom of mobility of residence.

- The right to the finest education man's social order can provide.

- And most importantly, the right to share fully in the governing councils of the state as equal members of the **body politic.**

To demand these God-given human rights is to seek black power, what I call audacious power—the power to build black institutions of splendid achievement.

audacious: recklessly bold and marked by great energy and originality.

debasing: degrading.

mediocrity: the state of being of ordinary or low quality.

subservience: holding an inferior, but useful, position to someone or something else.

discern: distinguish between, understand.

implement: achieve, accomplish.

body politic: a group of people who are politically organized under a single government.

Howard University was once well on its way toward becoming a lasting black institution of splendid achievement when it struggled to contain the intellectual excitement and dynamic creativity of such black scholars as Alain Locke, Sterling Brown, E. Franklin Frazier, Sam Dorsey, Eugene Holmes, James Nabrit and Rayford Logan—all on the campus at the same time. What glorious symbols they were of black creativity!

But where are the black symbols of creativity of 1966? Where is the greatness of our yesteryears? Where are the sonnets black poets once sung of the black man's agony of life? Can any good thing come out of Howard today?

There can and there must. I call today for a black **renaissance** at Howard University. **Resurrect** black creativity, not only in literature, history, law, poetry and English, but more so in mathematics, engineering, aerodynamics and nuclear physics. Like Nicodemus, Howard must be born again—born again in the image of black greatness gone before.

Will one black woman here today dare to come forth as a pilgrim of God, a **Sojourner Truth** [see entry]—as a black Moses, Harriet Tubman, or a Nannie Burroughs? Will one black man here today dare be a Denmark Vesey, a Nat Turner, a **Frederick Douglass** [see entry], a **Marcus Garvey** [see entry], a **W. E. B. Du Bois** [see entry] or a **Malcolm X** [see entry]?

One with God is a majority.

This divine oneness can restore Howard to the Glory of Charlie Houston whose classrooms were the womb of the civil rights movement—a womb that birthed a **Thurgood Marshall** [see entry]. But the womb has aborted and the good thing which must come out of Howard must also come out of black people. Ask yourselves that higher question: Can any good thing come of black people?

We are the last revolutionaries in America—the last transfusion of freedom into the bloodstream of democracy. Because we are, we must mobilize our wintry discontent to transform the cold heart and white face of this nation.

Indeed, we must "drop our buckets" where we are. We must stop blaming "whitey" for all our sins and oppressions and deal from situations with strength. Why sit down at the

renaissance: rebirth, reawakening.

resurrect: bring back to life.

Adam Clayton Powell, Jr.

bargaining table with the white man when you have nothing with which to bargain? Why permit social workers and various leagues and associations to represent us when they are representing the **decadent** white power structure which pays their salaries, their rent and tells them what to say? Such men cannot possess the noble **arrogance** of power that inspires men, moves nations and decides the fate of mankind.

I call for more arrogance of power among black people, but an arrogance of power that is God-inspired, God-led and God-daring....

We can cancel the captivity of our souls and destroy the enslavement of our minds by refusing to **compromise** any of our human rights. The era of compromise for the black man is gone! Birmingham, [Alabama, the scene of numerous violent civil rights demonstrations in 1963] Harlem and Watts [a black district of Los Angeles, California, that was rocked by a major race riot in August 1965] have proved this. You cannot compromise man's right to be free, nor can you sit down and "reason together" whether man should have some rights today and full rights tomorrow....

God calls us first to the conference table, and His Son, when the word of reason was no longer heeded, went into the temple and "began to cast out those that sold." Those that sell black people down the river must be cast out. Those conference tables which **defile** the human spirit must be overturned.

Conferences are for people who have time to **contemplate** the number of angels dancing on a civil rights pin. Conferences are for people who seek a postponement until tomorrow of a decision which screams for a solution today. Conferences are an extravagant orgy of therapy for the guilt-ridden and a purposeless exercise in **dialectics** for the lazy. America has been holding too many conferences, conducting too many seminars; writing too many books and articles about the black man and his right to freedom for over a century.

This week, three thousand black and white people will gather once again in our nation's capital to whisper words of **futility** into the hurricane of massive indifference. Certainly the federal government should cease to be a partner in this cruel, historic charade with the black man's rights.

decadent: corrupt.

arrogance: a feeling of superiority expressed boldly and with pride.

compromise: agree to give up certain rights or privileges in the interest of reaching a settlement acceptable to a group of people.

defile: disgrace, degrade.

contemplate: think or wonder about.

dialectics: an intellectual exchange of ideas.

futility: uselessness, ineffectiveness.

To fulfill these rights? Let us begin with first things first. The largest single employer in the United States is the federal government.... Yet, racial discrimination within the government—more **subtle,** more sophisticated, more elegantly structured—continues almost as rampant as yesterday. The times have changed, but the system hasn't.

Though racial persecution presses its crown of thorns on our brows, our faith in God must never falter. We must sustain that faith which helps us to cast off the **leprosy** of self-shame in our black skins and lift us up to the glorious healing power of belief in the excellence of black power. We must have the faith to build mighty black universities, black businesses and elect black men as governors, mayors and senators. Our faith must be sustained by our passion for dignity and our trust in God, not man's faithless reason in himself.

What is easier—"to say to the sick of the **palsy** 'Thy sins be forgiven thee'; or to say, 'Arise and take up thy bed and walk'?"

Black children of Howard, take up thy beds and walk into the new era of excellence.

Arise, and walk into a new spirit of black pride.

"Can there any good thing come out of Nazareth? Come and see, said Philip."

Nathanael came and saw Jesus and the world felt, as he did, the power of his love and the beauty of his words.

Can there any good thing come out of Howard University here today?

"Come and see," you Howard graduates must say. "Come and see" us erect skyscrapers of economic accomplishment, scale mountains of educational excellence and live among the stars of audacious political power.

"Come and see" us labor for the black masses—not the black leaders—but the black masses who have yearned for audacious leadership.

99

In March 1967, following an investigation into Powell's reported misbehavior in both his public and private life,

Adam Clayton Powell, Jr.

subtle: hidden, obscured.

leprosy: a morally or spiritually harmful influence (a meaning inspired by the disease of the same name that can result in severe physical deformities).

palsy: paralysis.

Powell leaving the House of Representatives, March 1967, after vote (later ruled unconstitutional) to expel him

*members of the House of Representatives voted to expel him. His Harlem **constituents** stood behind him, however. In a special election held that summer, they voted him back into office. After he agreed to give up his seniority and pay a fine for misuse of funds, he was finally allowed to take his seat again in January 1969. Six months later, the U.S.*

constituents: the people who elect someone to public office to represent them.

Supreme Court ruled that the House decision to expel him had been unconstitutional.

But Powell's career was nevertheless heading quickly toward its end. After being hospitalized for cancer in 1969, he was defeated in the 1970 Democratic primary. His death in 1972 sparked a few final headlines when two different women battled over his funeral arrangements and his estate. His body was ultimately cremated and his ashes were scattered over the island of Bimini in the Bahamas, one of Powell's favorite vacation spots.

Sources

Books

Baird, A. Craig, editor, *Representative American Speeches: 1949–1950,* Wilson, 1950.

Boulware, Marcus H., *The Oratory of Negro Leaders: 1900–1968,* Negro Universities Press, 1969.

Foner, Philip S., editor, *The Voice of Black America: Major Speeches by Negroes in the United States, 1797-1971,* Simon & Schuster, 1972.

Hamilton, Charles V., *Adam Clayton Powell, Jr.: The Political Biography of an American Dilemma,* Atheneum, 1991.

Haskins, James, *Adam Clayton Powell: Portrait of a Marching Black,* Dial, 1979.

Haygood, Wil, *Kings of Cats: The Life and Times of Adam Clayton Powell, Jr.,* Houghton, 1993.

Powell, Adam Clayton, Jr., *Keep the Faith, Baby!,* Trident, 1967.

Powell, Adam Clayton, Jr., *Adam by Adam: The Autobiography of Adam Clayton Powell, Jr.,* Dial, 1971.

Smith, Arthur L., *Rhetoric of Black Revolution,* Allyn & Bacon, 1969.

Williams, Jamye Coleman, and McDonald Williams, editors, *The Negro Speaks: The Rhetoric of Contemporary Black Leaders,* Noble & Noble, 1970.

Periodicals

Ebony, "Harlem Bids Farewell to Keeper of the Faith,", June 1972; "Adam Lives: Forever!," June, 1972, pp. 150-151.

Newsweek, "Black Revolution's Adam," April 17, 1972, p. 32.

New York Times, April 5, 1972.

Time, "Playboy Politician," April 17, 1972, p. 24.

Washington Post, April 6, 1972.

Colin Powell

1937–

Military and political leader

"I AM A DIRECT DESCENDENT OF ALL THE BLACK MEN AND WOMEN WHO SERVED THIS NATION IN UNIFORM FOR OVER THREE HUNDRED YEARS— ALL OF WHOM SERVED IN THEIR TIME AND IN THEIR WAY AND WITH WHATEVER OPPORTUNITY EXISTED THEN TO BREAK DOWN THE WALLS OF DISCRIMINATION AND RACISM TO MAKE THE PATH EASIER FOR THOSE OF US WHO CAME AFTER THEM."

One of the heroes to emerge from the Persian Gulf War (1990-1991) was General Colin Powell, the mastermind behind operations Desert Shield and Desert Storm. Americans who had lost nearly all faith in the military found a new reason to be proud as they came to know this man who rose up from humble beginnings to earn the trust of presidents. Well after retiring from the military, Powell remained one of the most respected public figures in the United States.

Early Life

Powell is the son of Jamaican immigrants who came to the United States in search of a better life. He was born in the Harlem district of New York City and grew up in the South Bronx. Throughout high school and later on at New York's City College he was an average student who wasn't especially interested in school. Outside the classroom, however, Powell excelled as a member of the college's Reserve

Officer Training Corps (ROTC) unit. (The ROTC offers a military-style program that prepares young people for positions in the U.S. Army Reserve.) He served as commander of the precision drill team and became cadet colonel, the highest possible rank. Upon his graduation in 1958 he went into the army, figuring he would put in his two years and then look for a "real" job.

Little did Powell know that his decision marked the beginning of a long and distinguished career that would eventually lead him into the upper levels of the United States government as an advisor to several presidents. Along the way came a series of increasingly important military assignments at home and abroad as well as several political appointments in Washington, D.C. Over time, Powell earned a reputation as a skilled and efficient organizer and mediator (someone who helps bridge the gap between two opposing sides) and as a leader of great integrity, honesty, and level-headedness.

Helps Restore the Reputation of the National Security Council

Most of Powell's early accomplishments occurred out of the public eye, either at various army bases or behind the scenes at the Pentagon (the building in Washington, D.C., that houses the offices of the U.S. Department of Defense). In 1986, however, at the personal request of President Ronald Reagan, Powell was named to a much higher-profile position—that of assistant to National Security Council (NSC) director Frank Carlucci.

Carlucci had been ordered to clean up the NSC and restore its credibility after its image was badly tarnished by the Iran-Contra scandal. This scandal had involved a complicated secret deal to win the release of American hostages in the Middle East by selling weapons to Iran. U.S. government officials linked to the NSC gave the profits from these arms sales to **right-wing** rebels, or contras, in the Central American country of Nicaragua who were trying to overthrow the **left-wing** Sandinista government. Powell's efforts to repair the NSC's reputation and establish controls to make sure nothing like the Iran-Contra scandal ever

right-wing: conservative; opposed to change or reform.

left-wing: liberal or radical in politics.

happened again were so impressive that he was chosen to replace his boss when Carlucci left to head the Department of Defense in late 1987. As further proof of Powell's high standing in Washington, his nomination received the enthusiastic approval of virtually every top government official.

Chairs Joint Chiefs of Staff

Powell served as head of the NSC throughout the rest of Reagan's term, then returned to military duty in early 1989. Later that year, however, President George Bush nominated him over dozens of other candidates to become chair of the Joint Chiefs of Staff (the main advisor to the president on military affairs—one of the most powerful positions in the U.S. government). Congress quickly confirmed him for the job, and in October 1989, Powell became the first African American and the youngest man ever to serve as the chair of the Joint Chiefs.

In August 1990, the Iraqi invasion of Kuwait moved Powell into the public eye as never before. His job required him to draw on his skills as a soldier, a politician, and a diplomat. For example, he planned the land, sea, and air campaigns the allies used to force Iraq to retreat. He also helped shape policy regarding nonmilitary matters. On top of all this, he had to sell the overall strategy to the president and to Congress and explain it to the American people.

Powell's appearances at a couple of televised press conferences won rave reviews. His calm and confident manner, his display of firmness without excessive boastfulness, and his obvious patriotism won him widespread respect and admiration. To many, he communicated a sense of decency lacking in many public figures and seemed to be the perfect example of the ideal military man, an image that had nearly been destroyed during the Vietnam War. Also appealing to most Americans was the impression Powell gave of having completely risen above society's many racial and political divisions.

Powell at Vietnam Veterans Memorial, Washington, D.C., 1991

Leaves Army after Thirty-Five Years of Service

As a result of his tremendous popular appeal, Powell faced countless questions after the Persian Gulf War about his political ambitions. For months, he carefully avoided saying anything that would have suggested he was seriously thinking about running for office. He even kept his political party preference a mystery. Instead, he finished out his term as chair of the Joint Chiefs of Staff in late 1993, toward the end of Bill Clinton's first year as president. He then retired from the military, having served both Democratic and Republican administrations with distinction.

Powell's retirement was a busy one. He spent quite a bit of time writing his memoirs, completing them in time for publication in late 1995. He has also accepted numerous invitations to speak before many different kinds of groups, especially young people.

One such appearance came on May 14, 1994, when he received an honorary degree from Howard University in Washington, D.C., and then delivered a speech to the graduating class. In his address, he touched on several of his favorite themes—the benefits of a good education, the need to persevere (continue) even in the face of hardship, the need to maintain a strong value system, and the need to take personal responsibility for one's life and one's actions. The following excerpt from his speech was provided by Powell's office.

I am so pleased to be with you on this very beautiful spring morning. I am deeply honored to be the recipient of an honorary degree....

I am especially pleased to be the commencement speaker for the class of 1994. I have wanted to be the commencement speaker for a number of years, and this is my lucky year.

Because you know, these days you get a lot of attention being a speaker at Howard University.... [Powell was referring here to an incident earlier in the school year when students invited a Nation of Islam official to speak on campus. Many people felt the school should not do anything that seemed to support the extremist views of the speaker, a close associate of the controversial head of the Nation of Islam, Louis Farrakhan.]

You know, the controversy over Howard's speaking policy has its positive side. It has caused the university to go through a process of self-examination, which is always a healthy thing to do. Since many people have been giving advice about how to handle this matter, I thought I might as well, too.

First, I believe with all my heart that Howard must continue to serve as an institution of learning excellence where freedom of speech is strongly encouraged and rigorously protected. That is at the very essence of a great university, and Howard is a great university.

And freedom of speech means permitting the widest range of views to be presented for debate, however controversial those views may be....

Some say that by hosting controversial speakers who shock our **sensibilities,** Howard is in some way promoting or endorsing their message. Not at all. Howard has helped put their message in perspective while protecting their right to be heard. So that the message can be exposed to the full light of day.

I have every confidence in the ability of the administration, the faculty and the students of Howard to determine who should speak on this campus.... I also have complete confidence in the students of Howard to make informed, educated judgments about what they hear.

But for this freedom to hear all views, you bear a burden to sort out wisdom from foolishness. There is great wisdom in the message of self-reliance, of education, of hard work, and of the need to raise strong families. There is utter foolishness, evil and danger in the message of hatred, or of **condoning** violence, however cleverly the message is packaged or entertainingly it is presented. We must find nothing to stand up and cheer about or applaud in a message of racial or ethnic hatred.

I was at the inauguration of President [Nelson] Mandela in South Africa earlier this week. You were there, too, by television and watched that remarkable event. Together, we saw what can happen when people stop hating and begin reconciling. [Former South African President F.W.] De Klerk the jailer became De Klerk the liberator and Mandela the prisoner became Mandela the president....

sensibilities: feelings.
condoning: excusing, approving.

Last week you also saw [Israeli] Prime Minister [Yitzhak] Rabin and PLO [Palestine Liberation Organization] Chairman Yasir Arafat sign another agreement on their still difficult, long road to peace, trying to end hundreds of years of hatred and two generations of violence....

In these two historic events, **intractable** enemies of the past have shown how you can join hands to create a force of moral authority more powerful than any army and which can change the world. Although there are still places of darkness in the world where the light of **reconciliation** has not penetrated, these two beacons of hope show what can be done when men and women of good will work together for peace and for progress.

There is a message in these two historic events for us assembled here today. As the world goes forward, we cannot start going backward.

African Americans have come too far and we have too far yet to go to take a detour into the swamp of hatred. We—as a people who have suffered so much from the hatred of others—must not now show tolerance for any movement or philosophy that has at its core the hatred of Jews or of anyone else. Our future lies in the philosophy of love and understanding and caring and building. Not of hatred and tearing down.

We know that. We must stand up for it and speak up for it! We must not be silent if we would live up to the legacy of those who have gone before us from this campus.

I have no doubt that this controversy will pass and Howard University will emerge even stronger, even more than ever a symbol of hope, of promise and of excellence. That is Howard's destiny!...

A few years ago ... I was involved in [a project] to build a memorial to the Buffalo Soldiers [see box], those brave black cavalrymen of the west whose **valor** had long gone unrecognized.... The Buffalo Soldiers were formed in 1867, at the same time as Howard University. It is even said that your mascot, the bison, came from the bison, or Buffalo, Soldiers.

Both Howard and the Buffalo Soldiers owe their early suc-

intractable: stubborn, not easily governed or ruled.

reconciliation: the state of being restored to friendship and harmony.

valor: bravery.

Colin Powell

The Buffalo Soldiers

After the Civil War, in which more than 35,000 black troops had lost their lives, Congress passed legislation to strengthen the nation's military forces. The legislation included the stipulation: "That to the six regiments of cavalry now in service shall be added four regiments, two of which shall be composed of colored men...." With that new law, the nation gained its first all-black Regular Army regiments: the 9th and 10th Cavalry, and the 24th and 25th Infantry—the "Buffalo Soldiers." Although the term "Buffalo Soldiers" originally referred to these four regiments, veterans of racially-segregated black army ground units of the 1860-1950 era have adopted the name.

Despite the change in the army's policy after the Civil War, the Buffalo Soldiers faced racial discrimination even as they risked their lives in the government's campaign against the Indians in the Plains during the late nineteenth century. For example, one of the original Buffalo Soldiers, Second Lieutenant Henry Ossian Flipper, was the first black to graduate from the United States Military Academy at West Point, New York, and he became the only black commissioned officer in the Regular Army. But Flipper was dismissed from the service on June 30, 1882, after a court martial in which he was convicted of conduct unbecoming an officer. A century later, his records revealed that he had been framed by his fellow officers. Only two other African Americans graduated from West Point in the nineteenth century and it was nearly fifty years after that before another black cadet would graduate from the United States Military Academy.

cess to the dedication and faith of white military officers who served in the Civil War. In Howard's case, of course, it was your namesake, Major General Oliver Howard. [Oliver Howard, a renowned Union general in the Civil War also known for later campaigns against Native Americans, was one of the founders and a president of Howard University. Howard was devoted to the cause of improving opportunities for black people after the Civil War and was the chief commissioner of the Freedman's Bureau, an agency designed to provide blacks with work, education, and fair treatment under the law during the Reconstruction Era in the South.] For the Tenth Cavalry Buffalo Soldiers, it was Colonel Benjamin Grierson who formed and commanded that regiment for almost twenty-five years. And he fought that entire time to achieve equal status for his black comrades. Together, Howard University and the Buffalo Soldiers showed what black Americans were capable of when given the education and opportunity, and when shown respect and when **accorded** dignity.

accorded: given, granted.

I am a direct descendent of those Buffalo Soldiers, of the Tuskegee Airmen [an all-black unit of fighter pilots in World War II trained at Tuskegee Institute and noted for their struggles against racial discrimination in the armed services] and of the Navy's "Golden Thirteen" [the first thirteen African Americans to be commissioned as officers in the U.S. Navy in 1944] the Montfort Point Marines, and all the black men and women who served this nation in uniform for over three hundred years—all of whom served in their time and in their way and with whatever opportunity existed then to break down the walls of discrimination and racism to make the path easier for those of us who came after them. I climbed on their backs and stood on their shoulders to reach the top of my chosen profession to become chairman of the American JCS [Joint Chiefs of Staff]. I will never forget my debt to them and to the many white Colonel Griersons and General Howards who helped me over the thirty-five years of my life as a soldier. They would say to me now, "Well done. And now let others climb up on your shoulders."

Howard's "Buffalo Soldiers" did the same thing and on their shoulders now stand governors and mayors and congressmen and generals and doctors and artists and writers and teachers and leaders in every segment of American society. And they did it for the class of 1994. So that you can now continue climbing to reach the top of the mountain while reaching down and back to help those less fortunate.

You face "great expectations." Much has been given to you and much is expected from you. You have been given a quality education, presented by a distinguished faculty who sit here today in pride of you. You have inquiring minds and strong bodies given to you by God and by your parents, who sit behind you and pass on to you today their still unrealized dreams and ambitions. You have been given citizenship in a country like none other on earth, with opportunities available to you like nowhere else on earth—beyond anything available to me when I sat in a place similar to this thirty-six years ago.

What will be asked of you is hard work. Nothing will be handed to you. You are entering a life of continuous study

Powell with troops, Gulf War, 1991

and struggle to achieve your goals. A life of searching to find that which you do well and love doing. Never stop seeking.

I want you to have faith in yourselves. I want you to believe to the depth of your soul that you can accomplish any task that you set your mind and energy to.

I want you to be proud of your heritage. Study your origins. Teach your children racial pride and draw strength and inspiration from the cultures of our **forebearers,** not as a way of drawing back from American society and its European roots, but as a way of showing that there are other roots as well.... To show that African Americans are more than a product of our slave experience. To show that our varied backgrounds are as rich as that of any other American; not better or greater, but

forebearers: ancestors.

Colin Powell | 293

every bit as equal. Our black heritage must be a foundation stone we can build on, not a place to withdraw into.

I want you to fight racism. But remember, as Dr. **[Martin Luther] King** [see entry] and Dr. Mandela have taught us, racism is a disease of the racist. Never let it become yours....

Racism is a disease you can help cure here by standing up for your rights and by your commitment to excellence and to performance. By being ready to take advantage of your rights and the opportunities that will come from those rights. Never let the dying hand of racism rest on your shoulder, weighing you down. Let racism always be someone else's burden to carry.

As you seek your way in the world, never fail to find a way to serve your community. Use your education and your success in life to help those still trapped in cycles of poverty and violence.

Above all, never lose faith in America. Its faults are yours to fix, not to curse.

America is a family. There may be differences and disputes in the family but we must not allow the family to be broken into warring factions. From the diversity of our people, let us draw strength and not cause weakness.

Believe in America with all your heart and soul and mind. It remains the "last best hope of earth." You are its inheritors and its future is today placed in your hands.

Go forth from this place today inspired by those who went before you.

Go forth with the love of your families and the blessings of your teachers.

Go forth to make this a better country and society. Prosper, raise strong families, remembering that all you will leave behind is your good works and your children.

Go forth with my humble congratulations. And let your dreams be your only limitations, now and forever....

In September 1994, Powell played a key role in a special three-member team President Bill Clinton sent to Haiti to persuade that country's ruling generals to step down and thus avoid an American invasion. His success touched off another round of **speculation** that he might be gearing up for a presidential bid in 1996. As usual, however, Powell declined to comment on his future plans.

The interest in Powell as a possible candidate for president increased throughout 1995. Polls continued to show that he was more popular than anyone else who had already announced an intention to run. While on a tour to promote his newly-published autobiography during the late summer and early fall, Powell hinted that he might be thinking of entering the race. As the year drew to a close, the question on nearly everyone's mind was, will he or won't he?

Finally, on November 8, 1995, Powell ended the suspense by declaring that he just didn't have the necessary "passion and commitment" to devote himself to politics at the moment. For the first time, he also revealed his preference for a specific political party—the Republicans. But Powell made it clear he was not in agreement with Republican **conservatives** on many social issues, especially abortion rights, affirmative action, and welfare reform.

Powell's announcement disappointed his supporters, but it did not completely end the guessing game about his future. As the nation geared up for the 1996 presidential election campaign, some people still hoped he might agree to run as an independent candidate or perhaps on the Republican ticket as the vice-presidential nominee. Powell himself rejected these ideas, but he has never ruled out the possibility that he might one day feel the "fire in the belly" he believes it takes to have a successful political career.

Sources

Books

Landau, Elaine, *Colin Powell: Four-Star General,* F. Watts, 1991.

Powell, Colin, *My American Journey: An Autobiography,* Random House, 1995.

speculation: the act of wondering or thinking about something, especially something about which one has little definite information.

conservatives: people who are moderate, cautious, inclined to follow tradition and reject or be suspicious of change.

Roth, David, *Sacred Honor: The Biography of Colin Powell,* Zondervan, 1993.

Woodward, Bob, *The Commanders,* Simon & Schuster, 1991.

Periodicals

Atlantic, "President Powell?" October 1993.

Ebony, "Black General at the Summit of U.S. Power," July 1988, pp. 136-146; "The World's Most Powerful Soldier," February 1990, pp. 136-142.

Esquire, "A Confederacy of Complainers," July 1991.

Newsweek, "'The Ultimate No. 2' for NSC," November 16, 1987, p. 63; "Pragmatist at the Pentagon," August 21, 1989, p. 20; "Bush's Maximum Force," September 3, 1990, pp. 36-38; "The Reluctant Warrior," May 13, 1991, pp. 18-22; "Everybody's Dream Candidate," August 23, 1993, p. 21; "Here We Go Again," September 26, 1994, pp. 20-24; "Can Colin Powell Save America?," October 10, 1994, pp. 20-26; "Powell on the Brink," November 6, 1995, pp. 36-39; "Moment of Truth," November 13, 1995, pp. 30-34; "Heartbreaker," November 20, 1995, pp. 36-41; "Why He Got Out," November 20, 1995, pp. 42-45.

People, "Colin Powell, America's Top Soldier, Has Taken His Influence from Harlem to the White House," September 10, 1990, pp. 52-55; "Colin Powell," December 31, 1990–January 7, 1991, pp. 60-61; "Colin Powell," spring/summer, 1991, pp. 38-39.

Time, "The General Takes Command," November 16, 1987, p. 22; "A 'Complete Soldier' Makes It," August 21, 1989, p. 24; "Five Who Fit the Bill," May 20, 1991, pp. 18-20; "The Rebellious Soldier," February 15, 1993, p. 32; "Colin Powell, the Reluctant Candidate," June 20, 1994, p. 15; "Beating the Doledrums," November 13, 1995, pp. 76-80; "General Letdown," November 20, 1995, pp. 48-57.

U.S. News and World Report, "The Right Stuff," February 4, 1991; "What's Next, General Powell?," March 18, 1991, pp. 50-53; "Colin Powell, Superstar: Will America's Top General Trade His Uniform for a Future in Politics?" September 20, 1993.

Deborah Prothrow-Stith

1954–

Physician and educator

One of the most passionate and respected voices speaking out on the subject of violence as a public health crisis is Dr. Deborah Prothrow-Stith, associate dean of the Harvard School of Public Health. In her many speeches as well as in her 1991 book, Deadly Consequences, *she paints a grim portrait of America. The nation's children, she says, are at tremendous risk of injury or worse because so many adults glorify violence and teach that force is an acceptable way to resolve conflicts. As a result, declares Prothrow-Stith, "a significant portion of our children are withering on the vine before they have even bloomed a little."*

Early Life and Career

A native of Texas, Prothrow-Stith received her bachelor's degree in 1975 from Spelman College in Atlanta, Georgia. She then went on to attend Harvard Medical School, from which she received her M.D. in 1979.

The problem of youth violence first began to trouble her

"FROM YOUR VERY FIRST CARTOON, ALL THE WAY THROUGH THE LATEST SUPERHERO MOVIE, WE HAVE TAUGHT YOU THAT VIOLENCE IS FUNNY, IT'S ENTERTAINING, IT'S THE HERO'S FIRST CHOICE, IT'S SUCCESSFUL, IT'S PAINLESS, IT'S GUILTLESS, IT'S INTERESTING."

deeply in 1978, the year she spent working as an intern in the emergency room of a hospital in Boston, Massachusetts. Her medical training had prepared her to care for the sick and the injured. And with a background in public health education, she was already inclined to think in terms of prevention as well as treatment of health problems. Yet she soon realized that while public health officials emphasized prevention in campaigns to reduce smoking and drug abuse, for example, they said nothing about violent behavior and its impact. "I wanted to understand the forces that sent so many [young men] to the emergency room—cut up, shot up, bleeding, and dead," she explained in a Detroit Free Press article. "Why were so many young males striking out with knives and guns? What could be done to stop the **carnage?** These questions motivated me to learn about violence."

Takes on Activist Role in Preventing Violence

Prothrow-Stith's search for answers eventually led her to become an activist in violence prevention. She insists that violence is truly a public health issue because it involves behavior that harms children and young people. Adolescent health is, in fact, Prothrow-Stith's medical specialty. During the late 1980s, she held several jobs in that field, including codirector of Boston's Health Promotion Center for Urban Youth, clinical chief of the Harvard Street Neighborhood Health Center, and commissioner of public health for the state of Massachusetts. (She was the first woman—and only the second African American—to fill the commissioner's post.) Prothrow-Stith has also served as an investigator on numerous adolescent violence projects. Since 1990, she has been associated with the Harvard School of Public Health.

Prothrow-Stith suggests that the way to eliminate violent behavior in American society is to teach people that there are ways other than force to deal with feelings of anger and aggression. This message, she says, should be spread by every means possible—government, schools, churches, community organizations, businesses, and the media. In this way, she hopes to end the cycle of child abuse and spouse abuse that often makes victims turn to violence themselves, either within the family or outside it.

carnage: killing.

Deborah Prothrow-Stith

Prothrow-Stith touches on these and related issues in many of her public appearances. She gives an average of three speeches a week, and her powerful words often leave her listeners in tears. In early May 1993, for example, she was in Chicago, Illinois, to address the United Methodist National Youth Ministry Organization conference on youth and violence. The following is an edited version of her keynote speech to an audience made up mostly of young adults. It is reprinted here from the June 1993 issue of Christian Social Action, *a publication of the United Methodist Church.*

66

I am a physician. During my training, I got a little tired of stitching people up and sending them out knowing that they were at risk of subsequent episodes of violence. In fact, the most painful thing I ever had to do was to go out and tell a family, who had sent their son off to school that morning expecting that he would return as usual that evening, that he was now dead. I got a little tired of this problem of violence and responding to it but not feeling as if, as a society, we were trying to do anything about it.

Then one morning about three a.m., a young man who had gone to a party came in because he had been in a fight, and he needed stitches just over his eyebrow. I put in the stitches and as he was about to leave, he turned to me and said, "Now look, don't go to bed because the person who did this to me is going to be in this emergency room in about an hour, and you are going to get all the practice you need putting in stitches."

I was struck by that because while I knew people were going out to fight again, they never really said that to me, and this night, this early morning, that young man told me what he was going to do. I did not have a response, because I wasn't trained as a physician to have a response.

It dawned on me that if he had made a suicide attempt, if he had taken pills, and we had cleaned out his stomach, and he said to us, "Don't go to bed because I'm going to go home and take some more pills, so I'll be back in this emergency room and you'll get all the practice you need cleaning out my stomach," we would have responded very differently. In fact, we wouldn't have waited on him to volunteer that information. If somebody is depressed or has made a suicide attempt, we are obligated to ask about his or her intentions.

The more I thought about it the more I realized that in almost every aspect of health care we were concerned about prevention. If somebody has heart disease, we might do surgery, or offer medicine. However, you know we also get involved in issues of behavior—diet, exercise, smoking, stress reduction—all to prevent future heart disease. With lead poisoning, a children's problem, we get the lead out of the blood. We do that, but we also make sure that the house has been de-leaded before the child goes home. That involves economic, political, and social issues. In the name of prevention, in almost every aspect of medicine, we are involved in those kinds of issues—behavioral, psychological, political, economic—except with this problem of violence, for which we were content to stitch people up and send them out.

I really started thinking about this problem of violence, and it dawned on me that part of the problem is that we don't think we can prevent violence. As a society, we act like violence is a natural part of the human mission, as if there is nothing we can do about it except get tough when it happens. So I started studying this problem of violence, and I learned a couple of things that I want to share with you.

The first thing I learned surprised me a little bit. I learned we have a very big problem in the United States. I guess I knew that because I read the newspapers and I watch television, but I was surprised at how we compared to other industrialized countries when it came to homicide rates. The homicide rate for young men in the United States is at about twenty-two per hundred thousand. We are four times higher than Scotland, the next highest industrialized country. We are seventy times higher than Austria, found at the bottom of the list. In the middle are Portugal, Greece, France, Canada, Israel—countries to which we usually compare ourselves, industrialized countries, not at war, with stable governments.

This information said to me that violence isn't a natural problem. If this was a natural or inevitable part of the human

Deborah Prothrow-Stith

condition, you would expect the homicide rate from country to country to be very similar. Everybody would have the problem. This kind of wide **discrepancy** in homicide rates suggested that we are doing something that we shouldn't be doing, or there are some things we ought to be doing that we are not doing, or both. Either way, this is a preventable problem; it is a problem we don't have to have.

I also learned that some people in the United States are at higher risk for this problem. The homicide rate for white men in the United States is over two times higher than Scotland and thirty-five times higher than Austria. You see, we think of this problem of violence as a problem of Black urban poor men, Hispanic men or "other" people, but we've got a U.S. problem. We have grown to tolerate a level of violence in the United States as normal that is so much higher than the rest of the world. However, there are some people who are more at risk. The homicide rate for young Black men in the United States is eighty-five per hundred thousand, four times higher than the rate that's already seventy times higher than the rate in Austria. We've got a problem in America and some people are at greater risk.

I need to tell you something about this. These data come from the FBI. That agency collects them regularly. They are labeled "Black," "white," and "other." So if you are a Latino man, for instance, you might be labeled "Black, " you might be labeled "white," you might be labeled "other." So there is a lot that this doesn't tell us.

Another thing that this doesn't tell us is about the problem of poverty. You read a lot of newspaper reports, a lot of social science reports, a lot of medical reports, that say Blacks have a higher problem of violence, but unless you consider the problem of poverty, you won't know what's race and what's poverty. All the studies that have been done that look at poverty say this problem is not race. It is labeled race, but young Black men are overrepresented among the poor. This is really poverty.

One study shows the homicide rate for young Black men in the military. That rate is lower than the homicide rate for white men in the United States, suggesting that being in the

discrepancy: difference.

military **affords** some economic, structural and support systems that affect this problem of violence.

Another study out of Atlanta looked at overcrowding in houses as a factor of poverty. Overcrowded whites had the same high homicide rates as did overcrowded Blacks, and less crowded Blacks had the same lower homicide rate as did less crowded whites. So [these studies] suggest that, while data are labeled race, what we are really looking at is poverty.

The second thing I learned shocked me. Again, using the FBI numbers, about half of the homicides occur between friends and families—people who know each other and get into an argument. Half of the murders in the United States occur among friends and families.

That shocked me because watching the news, reading the newspaper, gives a sense that stranger/bad-guy stuff is the bulk of the problem of violence and other felonies—that's drug trafficking, robbery, burglary, all that stranger/bad-guy stuff—that's fifteen percent of the homicides, and half occur between friends and family who get into an argument. Think about it. More police, more street lights, stiffer sentences, trying teenagers as adults—all of those responses to crime will not have an impact on two people who know each other who get into an argument.

We also know that they are often drinking alcohol, or using another drug, and we know they have a gun. Think about it. Two people who know each other, who are drinking alcohol, or using another drug, who get into an argument, and who have a gun, a handgun. That is the typical homicide setting. Family is twenty percent, and friends and acquaintances represent another forty percent, that's half of the time. People who know each other. We've got a growing problem with violence in part because our response to violence has little to do with the problem. We respond aggressively to that stranger/bad-guy stuff, but we do very little to prevent people who know each other who get into an argument from getting into a fight and from having homicide as an outcome.

Half the time hand guns are the weapon. When you think about the difference between the United States and all those other countries, think about guns. That is part of the problem. A very interesting study compared Seattle, Washington,

affords: provides.

302   Deborah Prothrow-Stith

to Vancouver, British Columbia—cities in two different countries, with two different sets of gun laws. In Vancouver, you cannot get a handgun legally. They are there, but much more difficult to get. In Seattle, as in the case in most of our cities, you can get a gun; and they are very accessible.

Look at the assault rate. In Seattle and Vancouver, assaults by sticks and bats and fists are about the same [numbers]; also about the same are assaults by knives. However, the assault by guns is about four times greater in Seattle than in Vancouver. People ask the question, "Do guns kill people, or do people kill people?" This study suggests that, in fact, guns play a big role.

The same study reported on homicides, not just assault, but homicides. In Seattle, homicides are five times higher than in Vancouver. Two people who know each other who get into an argument who don't have a gun don't seem to find another way to kill each other. Guns seem to be a major risk factor for this problem of homicide.

Think about the United States compared to other countries. Guns are part of the [violence] problem, but they're not all of the problem. Some countries with guns don't have our very high homicide rate. Scandinavian countries have two or three guns in almost every household because of the way people are enrolled in the military. Sweden is a country like that, and it doesn't have our high homicide rates.

What about poverty? Homicide rates are higher in poor communities in the United States, but this is not the poorest country in the world. Lots of countries are poorer and don't have our high homicide rates. The Atlanta study [indicates that] overcrowding is part of the problem. But if any of you have been to Hong Kong or plan to travel through the major cities in Japan, you'll see there are lots of places much more overcrowded than any U.S. city, and they don't have our high homicide rate. It's guns, and it's poverty, and it's overcrowding, and it is what I call our "make-my-day" ethic.

From your very first cartoon, all the way through the latest superhero movie, we have taught you that violence is funny, it's entertaining, it's the hero's first choice, it's successful, it's painless, it's guiltless, it's interesting. Some of you have been to enough funerals to know that it's not. It is not funny. It doesn't solve problems. It is certainly not a first choice. It is interesting because all of that hype in the movies about violence is just that—hype, not real. A lot of people make a lot of money making us think it is funny when somebody falls down or gets hit across the head or gets shot.

"Boyz N the Hood" was a movie that showed violence, but the violence didn't solve a problem. In actuality, "Boyz N the Hood" was kind of a sad movie, probably one of the few movies that told you the truth about violence.

In "Total Recall" not only did [the husband] shoot his wife, but after he shot her, he cracked a joke on the way out the door. In the escalator scene in that movie, he grabbed a man's body who had been shot and used that body to shield himself against the bullets as he went up the escalator. We were all thinking, "Wow, that is so smart." When he gets to the top of the escalator, he tosses that man to the side and said something like, "Buddy, you had a bad day." No funeral, no tears, no kids wondering why Daddy didn't come home, none of the pain of violence.

Part of our problem is this "make-my-day ethic." Movies and television are just part of it. We have had a "kick-butt" president, and we have had a "make-my-day" president. Adults in our society have gotten kind of confused on this issue. Sometimes parents tell kids, "You go back outside and you beat him up or I'm going to beat you." Nobody wants a wimp for a child.

It's not just the adults who are confused on this issue; teenagers put pressure on each other to fight. Somebody starts talking about somebody else. Somebody else tells somebody else, and somebody else tells somebody else, and then a whole bunch of somebodies want to know what's going on, what's going down, what's going to happen. Somebody says three o'clock on the corner and everybody's there. Everybody wants to see. With these whetted appetites for violence, we set our friends up to fight. Then we all go to see.

Something is really wrong with us as a country. Almost every message at almost every level of communication encourages violence. If our problem was stranger/bad-guy violence, then maybe I wouldn't care. But our problem is that we don't know how to get along with each other. We don't know how to get along with friends and family. Handling anger is not so easy, and right now we either beat people up or we do nothing.

I'm involved with a number of people across the country working to change this problem—change our attitudes about it, change our thinking on it. We are using some of what we used to change our attitudes about smoking. When I was about eight years old, I used to buy those candy cigarettes, and I would stand in front of the television and imitate all the beautiful people on television smoking. Movie stars smoked, everybody smoked. It was really a glamorous thing to do. Now, in Boston, people are standing outside in some very cold weather smoking cigarettes. You know why? Because it is offensive and it is unhealthy. Some of them work in smoke-free buildings. They can't smoke inside. That's a big change in attitude. It requires education, working with the media, doing lots of stuff to change our attitudes.

Two public service announcements now say, "Fighting is a lousy way to lose a friend. Friends for life. Don't let friends fight."

That's a part of this whole effort. It comes with t-shirts, billboards, posters, education in the classroom about handling anger. Probably the thing that keeps me most optimistic is how many students and parents have gotten involved in this. On the order of Mothers Against Drunk Driving (MADD), and Students Against Drunk Driving (SADD), there are organizations in Detroit called SOSAD (Save Our Sons and Daughters), in Atlanta called MOMS (Mothers of Murdered Sons) and in Nebraska, out of Omaha, called MAD DADS. These people are getting ready to say this is a problem that we don't have to have.

,,

Sources

Books

Prothrow-Stith, Deborah, with Michaele Weissman, *Deadly Consequences,* HarperCollins, 1991.

Periodicals

Christian Social Action, "Fighting Is a Lousy Way to Lose a Friend," June 1993.

Detroit Free Press, "A Bloody Turning Point," January 3, 1993, p. 6H; "Stop Glorifying Violence, Doctor Says," May 29, 1993, p. 10A.

Essence, January, 1992, p. 42.

People, June 14, 1993, p. 54.

Maria W. Miller Stewart

1803–1879

Journalist and women's rights activist

Although her career as a public speaker lasted less than two years, Maria W. Miller Stewart left a lasting mark on history. In 1832, for example, she became the first American-born woman to give a public speech. This was at a time when it was considered shocking for any woman to do such a thing. (Even more shocking in those days was the fact that she also spoke before a mixed audience of men and women.) In addition, Stewart was probably the first black woman to lecture on women's rights. And she was one of the early advocates of black pride, racial unity, and self-reliance.

Early Life

Stewart was a freeborn native of Hartford, Connecticut. Orphaned at the age of five, she was then bound (legally obligated to work for someone) to a minister's family. While she received virtually no formal schooling, she did manage to learn to read and write. (As an adult, she worked to

"METHINKS THERE ARE NO CHAINS SO GALLING AS THE CHAINS OF IGNORANCE—NO FETTERS SO BINDING AS THOSE THAT BIND THE SOUL, AND EXCLUDE IT FROM THE VAST FIELD OF USEFUL AND SCIENTIFIC KNOWLEDGE."

improve these skills.) She also picked up a knowledge of theology (the study of religious faith and practice) and how to speak and write on religious topics.

At the age of fifteen, Stewart left what had been her home to work elsewhere as a domestic servant. In 1826, she married James W. Stewart, an independent shipping agent based in Boston, Massachusetts. She and her husband then settled into a comfortable life as part of the city's small black middle class. But James Stewart died just three years into the marriage, and his wife was cheated out of a fairly large inheritance by a group of dishonest white businessmen and lawyers.

Alone as well as poor, Maria Stewart fell into a state of depression. After a long period during which she closely examined her own thoughts and feelings about life, she experienced a religious conversion. Stewart then vowed to devote the rest of her life to serving God and her race in the fight against oppression.

Launches Her Writing and Public Speaking Career

Stewart turned first to the written word to express her new-found activism. In late 1831, she contributed an essay to the Liberator, a weekly newspaper founded by the well-known **abolitionist** William Lloyd Garrison. He took a great interest in Stewart and went on to publish more of her work (including her speeches) in the Liberator.

In April 1832, Stewart began her public speaking career with an appearance before the Afric-American Female Intelligence Society in Boston. Her speeches blended her deep religious beliefs with a militant spirit of reform. Biblical figures, stories, and verses were sprinkled throughout, and she repeatedly urged her black listeners (especially black women) to take responsibility for strengthening themselves and their community. And while Stewart was a strong abolitionist, she did not make the fight against slavery the focus of her talks. Instead, she maintained that the greatest evils both free and enslaved African Americans had to face were racism, ignorance, and poverty.

abolitionist: a person in favor of getting rid of, or abolishing, slavery.

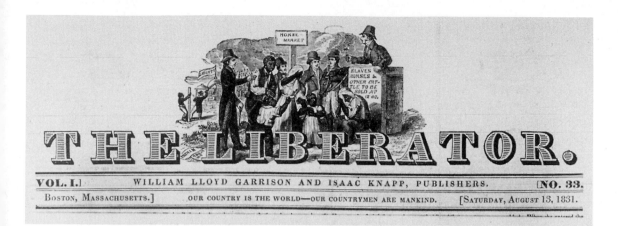

THE LIBERATOR.

VOL. I.]   WILLIAM LLOYD GARRISON AND ISAAC KNAPP, PUBLISHERS.   [NO. 33.

BOSTON, MASSACHUSETTS.]   OUR COUNTRY IS THE WORLD—OUR COUNTRYMEN ARE MANKIND.   [SATURDAY, AUGUST 13, 1831.

On September 21, 1832, Stewart stood before a mixed audience of men and women in Boston. An excerpt from this historic lecture follows. It is taken from the 1835 book Productions of Mrs. Maria W. Stewart, *which was later reprinted in* Spiritual Narratives, *Oxford University Press, 1988.*

Masthead of William Lloyd Garrison's antislavery newspaper, the Liberator

"

Why sit ye here and die? If we say we will go to a foreign land, the famine and the pestilence are there, and there we shall die. If we sit here, we shall die. Come let us plead our cause before the whites: if they save us alive, we shall live—and if they kill us, we shall but die.

Methinks I hear a spiritual **interrogation**—"Who shall go forward, and take off the **reproach** that is cast upon the people of color? Shall it be a woman?" And my heart made this reply—"If it is thy will, be it even so, Lord Jesus!"

I have heard much respecting the horrors of slavery; but may Heaven forbid that the generality of my color throughout these United States should experience any more of its horrors than to be a servant of servants, or **hewers** of wood and drawers of water! Tell us no more of southern slavery; for with few exceptions, although I may be very **erroneous** in my opinion, yet I consider our condition but little better than that. Yet, after all, methinks there are no chains so **galling** as the chains of ignorance—no **fetters** so binding

interrogation: question.
reproach: disgrace.
hewers: cutters.
erroneous: wrong.
galling: annoying.
fetters: chains, shackles.

Maria W. Miller Stewart   **309**

as those that bind the soul, and exclude it from the vast field of useful and scientific knowledge. O, had I received the advantages of early education, my ideas would, ere now, have expanded far and wide; but, alas! I possess nothing but moral capability—no teachings but the teachings of the Holy Spirit.

I have asked several individuals of my sex, who transact business for themselves, if providing our girls were to give them the most satisfactory references, they would not be willing to grant them an equal opportunity with others? Their reply has been—for their own part, they had no objection; but as it was not the custom, were they to take them into their employ, they would be in danger of losing the public **patronage.**

And such is the powerful force of prejudice. Let our girls possess what **amiable** qualities of soul they may; let their characters be fair and spotless as innocence itself; let their natural taste and **ingenuity** be what they may; it is impossible for scarce an individual of them to rise above the condition of servants. Ah! Why is this cruel and unfeeling distinction? Is it merely because God has made our complexion to vary? If it be, O shame to soft, relenting humanity! "Tell it not in Gath! Publish it not in the streets of Askelon!" Yet, after all, methinks were the American free people of color to turn their attention more **assiduously** to moral worth and intellectual improvement, this would be the result: prejudice would gradually diminish, and the whites would be compelled to say, unloose those fetters!

> Though black their skins as shades of night,
> Their hearts are pure, their souls are white.

Few white persons of either sex ... are willing to spend their lives and bury their talents in performing mean, **servile** labor. And such is the horrible idea that I **entertain** respecting a life of servitude, that if I conceived of there being no possibility of my rising above the condition of a servant, I would gladly hail death as a welcome messenger. O, horrible idea, indeed! To possess noble souls aspiring after high and honorable acquirements, yet confined by the chains of ignorance and poverty to lives of continual **drudgery** and toil. Neither do I know of any who have enriched themselves by spending their lives as house-domes-

patronage: support from customers.

amiable: likeable, pleasant.

ingenuity: cleverness, skill.

assiduously: carefully and persistently.

servile: lowly, demeaning.

entertain: keep in mind.

drudgery: boring and tiring work that offers little or no reward.

Maria W. Miller Stewart

tics.... I can but die but expressing my sentiments; and I am as willing to die by the sword as the **pestilence;** for I am a true born American; your blood flows in my veins, and your spirit fires my breast.

I observed a piece in the *Liberator* a few months since, stating that the **colonizationists** had published a work **respecting** us, asserting that we were lazy and idle. I **confute** them on that point. Take us generally as a people, we are neither lazy nor idle; and considering how little we have to excite or stimulate us, I am almost astonished that there are so many industrious and ambitious ones to be found; although I acknowledge, with extreme sorrow, that there are some who never were and never will be serviceable to society. And have you not a similar class among yourselves?

Again. It was asserted that we were "a ragged set, crying for liberty." I reply to it, the whites have so long and so loudly proclaimed the theme of equal rights and privileges, that our souls have caught the flame also, ragged as we are. As far as our merit deserves, we feel a common desire to rise above the condition of servants and drudges. I have learnt, by bitter experience, that continual hard labor deadens the energies of the soul, and **benumbs** the faculties of the mind; the ideas become confined, the mind barren, and, like the scorching sands of Arabia, produces nothing; or, like the uncultivated soil, brings forth thorns and thistles....

It is true, that the free people of color throughout these United States are neither bought nor sold, nor under the lash of the cruel driver; many obtain a comfortable support; but few, if any, have an opportunity of becoming rich and independent; and the employments we most pursue are as unprofitable to us as the spider's web or the floating bubbles that vanish into air. As servants, we are respected; but let us **presume** to aspire any higher, our employer regards us no longer....

I do not consider it **derogatory,** my friends, for persons to live out to service. There are many whose **inclination** leads them to aspire no higher; and I would highly commend the performance of almost any thing for an honest livelihood; but where **constitutional** strength is wanting, labor of this kind, in its mildest form, is painful. And doubtless

pestilence: disease.

colonizationists: people who supported the idea that American blacks should return to Africa and establish their own colony there.

respecting: about.

confute: strongly argue against.

benumbs: dulls, deadens.

presume: dare.

derogatory: tending to make seem inferior; disparaging.

inclination: personal preference.

constitutional: relating to one's physical build.

many are the prayers that have ascended to Heaven from Afric's daughters for strength to perform their work. Oh, many are the tears that have been shed for the want of that strength! Most of our color have dragged out a miserable existence of servitude from the cradle to the grave.

And what literary acquirements can be made, or useful knowledge derived, from either maps, books, or charts, by those who continually drudge from Monday morning until Sunday noon? O, ye fairer sisters, whose hands are never soiled, whose nerves and muscles are never strained, go learn by experience! Had we had the opportunity that you have had, to improve our moral and mental **faculties,** what would have **hindered** our **intellects** from being as bright, and our manners from being as dignified as yours? Had it been our lot to have been nursed in the lap of **affluence** and ease, and to have basked beneath the smiles and sunshine of fortune, should we not have naturally supposed that we were never made to toil? And why are not our forms as delicate, and our constitutions as slender, as yours? Is not the workmanship as curious and complete? Have pity upon us, have pity upon us, O ye who have hearts to feel for others' woes; for the hand of God has touched us. Owing to the disadvantages under which we labor, there are many flowers among us that are

—born to bloom unseen,
And waste their fragrance on the desert air.

My beloved brethren, as Christ has died **in vain** for those who will not accept of offered mercy, so will it be **vain** for the **advocates** of freedom to spend their breath in our behalf, unless with united hearts and souls you make some mighty efforts to raise your sons and daughters from the horrible state of servitude and **degradation** in which they are placed. It is upon you that woman depends; she can do but little besides using her influence: and it is for her sake and yours that I have come forward and made myself a **hissing** and a **reproach** among the people; for I am also one of the wretched and miserable daughters of the descendants of fallen Africa.

Do you ask, why are you wretched and miserable? I reply, look at many of the most worthy and interesting of us doomed to spend our lives in gentlemen's kitchens. Look at our young men, smart, active, and energetic, with souls filled

faculties: powers, abilities.

hindered: prevented.

intellects: minds.

affluence: wealth.

in vain: for no reason.

vain: useless, ineffective.

advocates: promoters, supporters.

degradation: having fallen to a lower level, condition, or status.

hissing: a target of sharp disapproval (that might be expressed by a hiss).

reproach: disgrace.

Maria W. Miller Stewart

with ambitious fire; if they look forward, alas! What are their prospects? They can be nothing but the humblest laborers, on account of their dark complexions; hence many of them lose their ambition, and become worthless. Look at our middle-aged men, clad in their rusty plaids and coats; in winter, every cent they earn goes to buy their wood and pay their rents; their poor wives also toil beyond their strength, to help support their families. Look at our aged **sires,** whose heads are whitened with the frosts of seventy winters, with their old wood-saws on their backs. Alas, what keeps us so? Prejudice, ignorance, and poverty.

But ah! Methinks our oppression is soon to come to an end; yea, before the Majesty of heaven, our groans and cries have reached the ears of the Lord of Sabaoth. As the prayers and tears of Christians will **avail** the finally **impenitent** nothing; neither will the prayers and tears of the friends of humanity avail us any thing, unless we possess a spirit of **virtuous emulation** within our breasts.

Did the pilgrims, when they first landed on these shores, quietly compose themselves, and say, "The Britons have all the money and all the power, and we must continue their servants forever?" Did they sluggishly sigh and say, "Our lot is hard, the Indians own the soil, and we cannot cultivate it?" No; they first made powerful efforts to raise themselves, and then God raised up those illustrious patriots, [George] Washington and [the Marquis de] Lafayette, to assist and defend them. And, my brethren, have you made a powerful effort? Have you prayed the legislature for mercy's sake to grant you all the rights and privileges of free citizens, that your daughters may rise to that degree of respectability which true merit deserves, and your sons above the service situations which most of them fill?

99

On September 21, 1833, Stewart delivered her farewell address to an audience in Boston. It is not known exactly why she decided to withdraw from public life, but it may have been because her outspokenness and her strong religious beliefs had made her the target of considerable criticism. In any event, before the end of the year she had left

sires: men.

avail: be of use, serve.

impenitent: people who are not sorry for the offenses they have committed.

virtuous emulation: morally pure ambition to become as good as or better than another person.

Boston for New York City. There she taught school for several years and joined two ladies' literary societies. These activities brought her into contact with some of the city's black **intellectuals.** *Later, she moved to Baltimore, Maryland, and then to Washington, D.C., where she spent the rest of her life.*

Sources

Books

Anderson, Judith, *Outspoken Women: Speeches by American Women Reformers, 1635-1935,* Kendall/Hunt, 1984.

Campbell, Karlyn Kohrs, *Man Cannot Speak for Her,* Volume 1: *A Critical Study of Early Feminist Rhetoric,* Volume 2: *Key Texts of the Early Feminists,* Greenwood Press, 1989.

Golden, James L., and Richard D. Rieke, *The Rhetoric of Black Americans,* Charles E. Merrill, 1971.

Lerner, Gerda, editor, *Black Women in White América: A Documentary History,* Pantheon Books, 1972.

Loewenberg, Bert James, and Ruth Bogin, editors, *Black Women in Nineteenth-Century American Life: Their Words, Their Thoughts, Their Feelings,* Pennsylvania State University Press, 1976.

Richardson, Marilyn, *Maria Stewart: America's First Black Woman Political Writer* (contains reprints of *Productions of Mrs. Maria W. Stewart* and *Meditations from the Pen of Mrs. Maria W. Stewart;* see below), Indiana University Press, 1971.

Spiritual Narratives (contains reprint of *Productions of Mrs. Maria W. Stewart*), Oxford University Press, 1988.

Stewart, Maria W. Miller, *Productions of Mrs. Maria W. Stewart,* Friends of Freedom and Virtue [Boston], 1835.

Stewart, Maria W. Miller, *Meditations from the Pen of Mrs. Maria W. Stewart,* [Washington, D.C.], 1879.

intellectuals: people known for their love of ideas and learning.

Mary Church Terrell

1863–1954

Educator and activist for women's rights and civil rights

Mary Church Terrell was an activist from the time she was in her twenties until almost her dying day at the age of ninety-one. She spoke out frequently about the problems blacks—especially black women—faced in American society. Her first crusade was against the brutal crime of lynching, an act of mob violence that involves putting someone to death, usually by hanging. Her final efforts were on behalf of the battle against racial segregation in Washington, D.C. In between, she worked tirelessly to advance the cause of women's rights.

Early Life

Mary Church was the daughter of the South's first black millionaire, Robert Church. He was a former slave who had made his fortune in real estate. His wife, Louisa Ayers, was a successful businesswoman in her own right.

Although her family lived in Memphis, Tennessee, young Mary attended school in Ohio. She went on to graduate from

"FOR FIFTEEN YEARS I HAVE RESIDED IN WASHINGTON, AND WHILE IT WAS FAR FROM BEING A PARADISE FOR COLORED PEOPLE, WHEN I FIRST TOUCHED THESE SHORES, IT HAS BEEN DOING ITS LEVEL BEST EVER SINCE TO MAKE CONDITIONS FOR US INTOLERABLE."

315

Oberlin College there, earning a bachelor's degree in 1884 and a master's degree in 1888. She then studied and traveled in Europe for two years. Against her father's wishes—he thought a young lady of her background should not work—she insisted on pursuing a career as a teacher. Her first job was as an instructor at Ohio's Wilberforce College (now University). She later taught in the District of Columbia public schools.

Following her marriage to fellow educator Robert Terrell in 1891, however, Mary had to give up her dream of a career. At that time, married women were legally prohibited from teaching. Instead, she became active in the women's suffrage (right to vote) movement. She also served as a founder and first president of the National Association of Colored Women. In addition, Terrell was a charter member of the National Association for the Advancement of Colored People (NAACP) and a member of the District of Columbia board of education. (She was, in fact, the first black woman in the country to hold such a position.)

Gains Worldwide Fame as a Lecturer

Terrell was much in demand as a lecturer in both the United States and Europe for nearly thirty years. She was an eloquent speaker who usually worked without notes. Most often, she talked to white audiences about such topics as racial injustice, lynching, the progress of black women since Emancipation, women's suffrage, and black history and culture. Since she firmly believed that racism springs from ignorance, she made a point of trying to educate her audiences and open their eyes to the world as African Americans experienced it.

Especially disturbing to Terrell was the fact that her home of Washington, D.C., was one of the most segregated cities in the country. In her view, the existence of such discrimination in the nation's capital was a disgrace to the ideals upon which the United States had been founded. Thus, she was for many years a leader in the district's fight against Jim Crowism (see box on page 318).

On October 10, 1906, Terrell spoke at a meeting of the United Women's Club of Washington, D.C. Her talk focused on what African Americans routinely had to deal with as district residents. Her remarks appeared in the January 24, 1907, issue of the Independent. *They were later reprinted in* Man Cannot Speak for Her, *Volume 2:* Key Texts of the Early Feminists, *by Karlyn Kohrs Campbell, Greenwood Press, 1989, from which this version is taken.*

"

Washington, D.C., has been called "The Colored Man's Paradise." Whether this **sobriquet** was given to the national capital in bitter **irony** by a member of the handicapped race, as he reviewed some of his own persecutions and **rebuffs,** or whether it was given immediately after the war by an ex-slaveholder who for the first time in his life saw colored people walking about like freemen, minus the overseer and his whip, history saith not. It is certain that it would be difficult to find a worse **misnomer** for Washington than "The Colored Man's Paradise" if so **prosaic** a consideration as **veracity** is to determine the appropriateness of a name.

For fifteen years I have resided in Washington, and while it was far from being a paradise for colored people, when I first touched these shores, it has been doing its level best ever since to make conditions for us intolerable. As a colored woman I might enter Washington any night, a stranger in a strange land, and walk miles without finding a place to lay my head. Unless I happened to know colored people who live here or ran across a chance acquaintance who could recommend a colored boarding-house to me, I should be obliged to spend the entire night wandering about. Indians, Chinamen [sic], Filipinos, Japanese and representatives of any other dark race can find hotel accommodations, if they can pay for them. The colored man alone is thrust out of the hotels of the national capital like a leper.

As a colored woman I may walk from the Capitol to the White House, ravenously hungry and abundantly supplied with money with which to purchase a meal, without finding a single restaurant in which I would be permitted to take a morsel of food, if it was patronized by white people, unless I were willing to sit behind a screen. As a colored woman I cannot visit the tomb of the Father of this country, which

sobriquet: nickname.

irony: sarcastically saying one thing when the opposite is actually true.

rebuffs: rejections.

misnomer: incorrect or improper name.

prosaic: ordinary.

veracity: truthfulness, correctness.

Jim Crowism or Jim Crow Laws

Beginning in the 1880s, many Southern states began to pass laws calling for strict separation of the races. These laws discriminated against African Americans in virtually all areas of public life, from schools and transportation to restaurants and hotels. "Jim Crow" was a character in a song that had been popular during the 1830s, and the term was often used to refer to blacks. Thus, "Jim Crowism" or "Jim Crow Laws" described all practices—whether approved by law or by tradition—that involved discriminatory treatment of blacks.

In 1896, the U.S. Supreme Court declared such laws constitutional in the famous *Plessy* v. *Ferguson* case. The decision upheld the state of Louisiana's right to segregate railroad cars. The Court maintained that the constitution only guaranteed political equality, not social equality, and that "separate but equal" facilities were acceptable.

owes its very existence to the love of freedom in the human heart and which stands for equal opportunity to all, without being forced to sit in the Jim Crow section of an electric car which starts from the very heart of the city—midway between the Capitol and the White House. If I refuse thus to be humiliated, I am cast into jail and forced to pay a fine for violating the Virginia laws. Every hour in the day Jim Crow cars filled with colored people, many of whom are intelligent and well-to-do, enter and leave the national capital.

As a colored woman I may enter more than one white church in Washington without receiving that welcome which as a human being I have a right to expect in the sanctuary of God. Sometimes the color blindness of the usher takes on that peculiar form which prevents a dark face from making any impression whatsoever upon his retina, so that it is impossible for him to see colored people at all. If he is not so afflicted, after keeping a colored man or woman waiting a long time, he will ungraciously show these dusky Christians who have had the **temerity** to thrust themselves into a temple where only the fair of face are expected to worship God to a seat in the rear, which is named in honor of a certain personage, well known in this country, and commonly called Jim Crow.

Unless I am willing to engage in a few menial occupations, in which the pay for my services would be very poor, there is no way for me to earn an honest living, if I am not a trained

temerity: boldness.

nurse or a dressmaker or can secure a position as teacher in the public schools, which is exceedingly difficult to do. It matters not what my intellectual **attainments** may be or how great is the need of the services of a competent person, if I try to enter many of the numerous vocations in which my white sisters are allowed to engage, the door is shut in my face.

From one Washington theater I am excluded altogether. In the remainder certain seats are set aside for colored people, and it is almost impossible to secure others....

If I possess artistic talent, there is not a single art school of repute which will admit me....

With the exception of the Catholic University, there is not a single white college in the national capital to which colored people are admitted, no matter how great their ability, how lofty their ambition, how unexceptionable their character or how great their thirst for knowledge may be.

Not only can colored women secure no employment in the Washington stores, department and otherwise, except as menials, and such positions, of course, are few, but even as customers they are not infrequently treated with discourtesy both by the clerks and the proprietor himself.....

In one of the Washington theaters from which colored people are excluded altogether, members of the race have been viciously assaulted several times, for the proprietor well knows that colored people have no **redress** for such discriminations against them in the District courts....

Altho [sic] white and colored teachers are under the same Board of Education and the system for the children of both races is said to be **uniform,** prejudice against the colored teachers in the public schools is manifested in a variety of ways.... No matter how competent or superior the colored teachers in our public schools may be, they know that they can never rise to the height of a directorship, can never hope to be more than an assistant and receive the meager salary therefor, unless the present regime is radically changed....

Strenuous efforts are being made to run Jim Crow streetcars in the national capital. "Resolved, that a Jim Crow law should be adopted and enforced in the District of Columbia," was the subject of a discussion engaged in last January by the

attainments: achievements.

redress: compensation, a way of righting a wrong done to someone.

uniform: equal, identical.

Columbian Debating Society of the George Washington University in our national capital, and the decision was rendered in favor of the affirmative. Representative Heflin, of Alabama, who introduced a bill providing for Jim Crow street cars in the District of Columbia last winter, has just received a letter from the president of the East Brookland Citizens' Association "indorsing [sic] the movement for separate street cars and sincerely hoping that you will be successful in getting this enacted into a law as soon as possible." Brookland is a suburb of Washington.

The colored laborer's path to a decent livelihood is by no means smooth. Into some of the trades unions here he is admitted, while from others he is excluded altogether. By the union men this is denied, altho [sic] I am personally acquainted with skilled workmen who tell me they are not admitted into the unions because they are colored. But even when they are allowed to join the unions they frequently **derive** little benefit, owing to certain tricks of the trade. When the word passes round that help is needed and colored laborers apply, they are often told by the union officials that they have secured all the men they needed, because the places are reserved for white men, until they have been provided with jobs, and colored men must remain idle, unless the supply of white men is too small....

And so I might go on citing instance after instance to show the variety of ways in which our people are sacrificed on the altar of prejudice in the Capital of the United States and how almost insurmountable are the obstacles which block his [sic] path to success. Early in life many a colored youth is so appalled by the helplessness and the hopelessness of his situation in this country that, in a sort of stoical despair he resigns himself to his fate. "What is the good of our trying to acquire an education? We can't all be preachers, teachers, doctors and lawyers. Besides those professions, there is almost nothing for colored people to do but engage in the most menial occupations, and we do not need an education for that." More than once such remarks, uttered by young men and women in our public schools who possess brilliant intellects, have wrung my heart.

It is impossible for any white person in the United States, no matter how sympathetic and broad, to realize what life

derive: obtain.

Mary Church Terrell

would mean to him if his **incentive** to effort were suddenly snatched away. To the lack of incentive to effort, which is the awful shadow under which we live, may be traced the wreck and ruin of scores of colored youth. And surely nowhere in the world do oppression and persecution based solely on the color of the skin appear more hateful and hideous than in the capital of the United States, because the **chasm** between the principles upon which this government was founded, in which it still **professes** to believe, and those which are daily practiced under the protection of the flag, yawns so wide and deep.

, ,

Terrell's battle against segregation in Washington continued throughout the rest of her life. During the early 1950s, when she was nearly ninety, she achieved one of her final victories. The protest she headed involved a group of blacks who had demanded that district officials enforce an old law banning restaurants from discriminating against customers on the basis of race as long as they were "well behaved." In June 1953, the U.S. Supreme Court ruled in favor of the old law. The Court's decision thus paved the way for the integration of other public facilities in the capital.

Sources

Books

Boulware, Marcus H., *The Oratory of Negro Leaders: 1900-1968,* Negro Universities Press, 1969.

Campbell, Karlyn Kohrs, editor, *Man Cannot Speak for Her,* Volume 1: *A Critical Study of Early Feminist Rhetoric,* Volume 2: *Key Texts of the Early Feminists,* Greenwood Press, 1989,

Foner, Philip S., editor, *The Voice of Black America: Major Speeches by Negroes in the United States, 1797-1971,* Simon & Schuster, 1972.

Jones, Beverly Washington, *Quest for Equality: The Life and Writings of Mary Church Terrell,* Carlson Publishers, 1990.

Terrell, Mary Church, *A Colored Woman in a White World* (reprint), Arno, 1980.

incentive: motivation.
chasm: a deep, wide space.
professes: claims.

Clarence Thomas

1948–

Associate justice of the U.S. Supreme Court

Clarence Thomas was an inexperienced and little-known federal appeals court judge when President George Bush nominated him on July 1, 1991, to replace retiring U.S. Supreme Court Justice **Thurgood Marshall** *(see entry). But within just a few weeks, he became the target of widespread criticism for his conservative political views. And before his confirmation hearings (meetings held to help determine if he was the right person to hold the position) finally ended in October, he had become tangled in an explosive national controversy involving what some have called the most important workplace issue of the 1990s: sexual harassment. (Sexual harassment is annoyance of a sexual nature that is intended to embarrass, frighten, or threaten someone.)*

Early Life

A native of the small Georgia town of Pin Point, Thomas grew up in what he has described as a "strong, stable, and conservative" household. The major influences on his life during early childhood were his maternal grandparents (his mother's parents). He and his younger brother lived with them after the Thomas family home burned down around 1955. Later in his youth, Thomas received additional support and encouragement from the white nuns who ran the all-black Catholic elementary school he attended.

*Thomas completed his high school education at a Catholic boarding school in rural Georgia. He then entered Missouri's Immaculate Conception Seminary with the goal of becoming a priest. But the 1968 assassination of **Martin Luther King, Jr.** (see entry) made him think twice about his plans.*

Later that year, Thomas left the seminary and transferred to Holy Cross College in Massachusetts, where he earned his bachelor's degree in 1971. He then headed to Yale University Law School. Following his graduation in 1974, he went to work as an aide to Missouri Attorney General John Danforth. Three years later he quit that job to serve as an attorney for the Monsanto Company in St. Louis, Missouri. When Danforth was elected to the U.S. Senate in 1979, Thomas resigned from Monsanto and moved to Washington, D.C., to work for his former boss.

In Washington, Thomas slowly began to make a name for himself in Republican circles as an up-and-coming black conservative. He wrote several articles and gave a few speeches condemning welfare, school desegregation, affirmative action, and abortion. Eventually, he attracted the attention of officials in the administration of President Ronald Reagan. In May 1981, Thomas was named assistant secretary for civil rights in the Department of Education. Eight months later, he was chosen to head the Equal Employment Opportunity Commission (EEOC). The EEOC investigates job discrimination complaints involving race, sex, color, religion, or national origin.

In late 1989, President Bush nominated Thomas for a judgeship on the U.S. Circuit Court of Appeals for Washington, D.C. He was easily confirmed (approved) by the Senate Judiciary Committee in March 1990. Over the next sixteen months, he issued decisions in only a couple of dozen routine cases. Nevertheless, on July 1, 1991, President Bush named Thomas to replace U.S. Supreme Court Justice Thur-good Marshall, who had decided to retire for health reasons.

Reaction to the nomination was swift and fairly negative during the weeks before Senate confirmation hearings began in September 1991. Members of a number of civil rights organizations and women's groups expressed concern and sometimes outrage that an "ultraconservative" like Thomas would be taking the place of one of the Court's most liberal members. Others pointed to his lack of experience as a judge as reason enough to find him unacceptable for the job.

Despite these criticisms, Thomas won over the Senate Judiciary Committee and appeared to be headed for full Senate approval until October 6. On that day, a startling piece of information was leaked to the media. According to news reports, a University of Oklahoma law professor named Anita Hill (see box, pp. 326–327) had provided Judiciary Committee staff members with a confidential statement back in September. In her statement, she claimed that Thomas had sexually harassed her during the early 1980s when she worked for him at the Department of Education and later at the EEOC. This accusation touched off an uproar throughout the country. Many people demanded that Hill be given a chance to tell her side of the story to the American public. Reluctantly, the Judiciary Committee agreed to resume the hearings.

On October 11, 1991, a nationwide television audience watched and listened closely as Hill stated calmly and in detail how Thomas had made numerous sexual advances toward her. She also noted that he had frequently tried to involve her in lewd (vulgar or obscene) conversations about **pornographic** *movies.*

Thomas responded to her charges with a mixture of anger and confusion. He spoke first at a morning session before Hill had testified and later at an evening session that followed her appearance before the Judiciary Committee. Excerpts from his remarks are reprinted here from the official U.S. government **transcript** *of the hearings. The document is entitled* Nomination of Judge Clarence Thomas

pornographic: intended to cause sexual excitement.

transcript: a typewritten copy of spoken or recorded material.

Clarence Thomas

to Be Associate Justice of the Supreme Court of the United States: Hearings Before the Committee on the Judiciary, United States Senate, *102nd Congress, 1st session, Part 4 of 4 parts, October 11, 12, and 13, 1991, pp. 5-10, 157-158, U.S. Government Printing Office, 1993.*

66

Mr. Chairman, Senator [Strom] Thurmond, members of the committee: as excruciatingly difficult as the last two weeks have been, I welcome the opportunity to clear my name today....

The first I learned of the **allegations** by Professor Anita Hill was on September 25, 1991, when the FBI came to my home to investigate.... When informed by the FBI agent of the nature of the allegations and the person making them, I was shocked, surprised, hurt, and enormously saddened.

I have not been the same since that day. For almost a decade my responsibilities included enforcing the rights of victims of sexual harassment. As a boss, as a friend, and as a human being I was proud that I have never had such an allegation leveled against me....

In addition, several of my friends, who are women, have confided in me about the horror of harassment on the job, or elsewhere. I thought I really understood the anguish, the fears, the doubts, the seriousness of the matter....

I have been wracking my brains, and eating my insides out trying to think of what I could have said or done to Anita Hill to lead her to allege that I was interested in her in more than a professional way, and that I talked with her about pornographic or x-rated films.

Contrary to some press reports, I **categorically** denied all of the allegations and denied that I ever attempted to date Anita Hill, when first interviewed by the FBI. I strongly **reaffirm** that denial. Let me describe my relationship with Anita Hill.

In 1981, after I went to the Department of Education as an assistant secretary in the Office of Civil Rights, one of my closest friends ... brought Anita Hill to my attention. As I remember, he indicated that she was dissatisfied with her law

allegations: claims, charges.
categorically: absolutely.
reaffirm: declare positively once again.

Anita Hill

(1956—)

The youngest of thirteen children born to an Oklahoma farm couple, Anita Hill grew up in an atmosphere where both education and Baptist religious traditions were very important. In 1981, not long after receiving her law degree from Yale University, she joined the civil rights division of the U.S. Department of Education. There her supervisor was Clarence Thomas. Within just a few months, he left for a new government job as head of the Equal Employment Opportunity Commission (EEOC). Hill accompanied Thomas to the EEOC and continued to work for him until 1983, when she moved back to Oklahoma. In 1986, she became a law professor at the University of Oklahoma.

Five years later, Hill's dramatic testimony before the Senate Judiciary Committee accusing her former boss of sexual harassment forced a nation to choose between two respected, believable people with very different stories to tell. Some accused Hill of trying to ruin Thomas's life for personal reasons. Others expressed sympathy and understanding and criticized those who doubted her truthfulness and questioned her character. For many blacks, race was as important as sex in the controversy because a black woman had made accusations that threatened to destroy the career and reputation of a black man. Black women in particular had to decide which was more important—loyalty to one's race or to one's gender.

In recognition of the courage it took for her to go public with her charges against Thomas, Hill has been showered with honors. On August 9, 1992, for example, the American Bar Association Commission on Women in the Profession presented her with a special award. In her acceptance speech, Hill discussed why women from all walks of life (but especially professional women) should be concerned about sexual harassment.

Hill said that professional women who have "made it" in their fields—that is, who are considered successful and productive—should consider two modern-day misperceptions about women that she had to face at the confirmation hearings and that all women who file sexual harassment claims are likely to confront.

"The first is the premise that no woman can be presumed to be telling the truth

firm and wanted to work in government. Based primarily, if not solely, on [his] recommendation, I hired Anita Hill.

During my **tenure** at the Department of Education, Anita Hill was an attorney-adviser who worked directly with me.... I recall being pleased with her work product and the professional, but **cordial** relationship which we enjoyed at work. I also recall engaging in discussions about politics and current events.

Upon my nomination to become chairman of the Equal

tenure: time in office.
cordial: friendly.

Clarence Thomas

about her experiences of sexual abuse. Even without apparent motives, [everyone thinks that] women will lie, fantasize or delude themselves....

"The second premise is that a woman's contribution to the workplace never outweighs that of the man.... Wrapped up neatly in the harassment issue ... are questions about our integrity and our professional work. And the burden of proof [the responsibility for proving a charge] in the court of popular opinion seems always to be on us....

"We as women who have made it may comfortably distance ourselves from these experiences of the victims and their plight. We may bolster [prop up] our distancing with assumptions about ages and level of education.... We can conclude that we are different.

"But when the issue is sexual harassment we must face it squarely, for it is neither removed from us culturally and socially nor is it a historic relic. It is real in our lives and in the lives of others....

"From the slave to the domestic servant, from factory worker to construction worker, from law professor to neurosur-

geon, we are each the potential target of this kind of abuse of power...."

After the confirmation, Hill generally remained out of the public eye. She did not give many interviews, and only now and then agreed to give a speech, usually to legal groups, women's organizations, or students. After taking a leave of absence from her teaching job at the University of Oklahoma, she returned to the classroom in the fall of 1995. She reportedly used the time off to write her autobiography as well as a book on sexual harassment.

Employment Opportunity Commission, Anita Hill, to the best of my **recollection,** assisted me in the nomination and confirmation process. After my confirmation, she ... joined me at EEOC. I do not recall that there was any question or doubts that she would become a special assistant to me at EEOC, although as a career employee she retained the option of remaining at the Department of Education.

At EEOC our relationship was more distant. And our contacts less frequent, as a result of the increased size of my per-

recollection: memory.

sonal staff and the dramatic increase and **diversity** of my day-to-day responsibilities.

Upon reflection, I recall that she seemed to have had some difficulty adjusting to this change in her role. In any case, our relationship remained both cordial and professional. At no time did I become aware, either directly or indirectly that she felt I had said, or done anything to change the cordial nature of our relationship.... I am certain that had any statement or conduct on my part been brought to my attention, I would remember it clearly.... But there were no such statements.

In the spring of 1983, Mr. Charles Cothey contacted me to speak at the law school at Oral Roberts University in Tulsa, Oklahoma. Anita Hill, who is from Oklahoma, accompanied me on that trip ... primarily because this was an opportunity to combine business and a visit to her home.

As I recall, during our visit at Oral Roberts University, Mr. Cothey mentioned to me the possibility of approaching Anita Hill to join the faculty at Oral Roberts University Law School. I encouraged him to do so. I noted to him, as I recall, that Anita Hill would do well in teaching. I recommended her highly and she eventually was offered a teaching position.

Although I did not see Anita Hill often after she left EEOC, I did see her on one or two subsequent visits to Tulsa, Oklahoma.... I also occasionally received telephone calls from her....

Throughout the time that Anita Hill worked with me I treated her as I treated my other special assistants. I tried to treat them all cordially, professionally, and respectfully. And I tried to support them in their endeavors, and be interested in and supportive of their success.

I had no reason or basis to believe my relationship with Anita Hill was anything but this way until the FBI visited me a little more than two weeks ago. I find it particularly troubling that she never raised any hint that she was uncomfortable with me....

And to my fullest knowledge, she did not speak to any other women working with or around me, who would feel

diversity: variety.

Clarence Thomas: "I will not allow this committee or anyone else to probe into my private life. This is not what America is all about."

comfortable enough to raise it with me.... Nor did she raise it with mutual friends....

The fact that I feel so very strongly about sex harassment and spoke loudly about it at EEOC has made these allegations doubly hard on me. I cannot imagine anything that I said or did to Anita Hill that could have been mistaken for sexual harassment.

But with that said, if there is anything that I have said that has been **misconstrued** by Anita Hill or anyone else, to be sexual harassment, then I can say that I am so very sorry and I wish I had known. If I did know I would have stopped immediately and I would not, as I have done over the past two weeks, had to tear away at myself trying to think of what I could possibly have done. But I have not said or done the things that Anita Hill has alleged. God has gotten me through the days since September 25 and He is my judge.

Mr. Chairman, something has happened to me in the dark days that have followed since the FBI agents informed me about these allegations. And the days have grown darker, as this very serious, very explosive, and very sensitive allegation or these sensitive allegations were selectively leaked, in a **distorted** way to the media over the past weekend.

As if the confidential allegations, themselves, were not enough, this apparently **calculated** public disclosure has caused me, my family, and my friends enormous pain and great harm.

I have never, in all my life, felt such hurt, such pain, such agony.... During the past two weeks, I lost the belief that if I did my best all would work out. I called upon the strength that helped me get here from Pin Point, and it was all **sapped** out of me. It was sapped out of me because Anita Hill was a person I considered a friend, whom I admired and thought I had treated fairly and with the utmost respect. Perhaps I could have better weathered this if it were from someone else, but here was someone I truly felt I had done my best with....

When I stood next to the president ... being nominated to the Supreme Court of the United States, that was a high honor. But as I sit here, before you, 103 days later, that honor has been crushed. From the very beginning charges were leveled against me from the shadows....

I have **complied** with the rules. I responded to a document request that produced over 30,000 pages of documents. And I have testified for 5 full days, under oath. I have endured this ordeal for 103 days. Reporters sneaking into my garage to examine books I read. Reporters and interest groups swarming over divorce papers, looking for dirt. Unnamed people starting **preposterous** and damaging rumors. Calls

misconstrued: misunderstood.

distorted: twisted, misleading.

calculated: carefully and deliberately planned.

sapped: drained.

complied: followed, obeyed.

preposterous: outrageous, ridiculous.

Clarence Thomas

all over the country specifically requesting dirt. This is not American. This is Kafka-esque. [Franz Kafka was a Czech writer known for his nightmarish view of modern life in which man is at the mercy of unknown forces beyond his control or understanding.] It has got to stop. It must stop for the benefit of future nominees, and our country. Enough is enough.

I am not going to allow myself to be further humiliated in order to be confirmed. I am here specifically to respond to allegations of sex harassment in the workplace. I am not here to be further humiliated by this committee, or anyone else, or to put my private life on display for a **prurient** interest or other reasons. I will not allow this committee or anyone else to probe into my private life. This is not what America is all about....

Mr. Chairman, in my forty-three years on this Earth, I have been able, with the help of others and with the help of God, to defy poverty, avoid prison, overcome segregation, bigotry, racism, and obtain one of the finest educations available in this country. But I have not been able to overcome this process. This is worse than any obstacle or anything that I have ever faced.....

Mr. Chairman, I am proud of my life, proud of what I have done, and what I have accomplished, proud of my family, and this process, this process is trying to destroy it all. No job is worth what I have been through, no job. No horror in my life has been so **debilitating.** Confirm me if you want, don't confirm me if you are so led, but let this process end. Let me and my family regain our lives. I never asked to be nominated. It was an honor. Little did I know the price, but it is too high....

Instead of understanding and appreciating the great honor bestowed upon me, I find myself, here today defending my name, my **integrity,** because somehow select portions of confidential documents dealing with this matter were leaked to the public.

Mr. Chairman, I am a victim of this process and my name has been harmed, my integrity has been harmed, my character has been harmed, my family has been harmed, my friends have been harmed. There is nothing this committee, this

prurient: marked by an excessive interest in something (especially of a sexual nature) considered unwholesome or unusual.

debilitating: crippling.

integrity: honesty, firm belief in following high moral standards.

body or this country can do to give me my good name back, nothing.

I will not provide the rope for my own **lynching** or for further humiliation. I am not going to engage in discussions, nor will I submit to roving questions of what goes on in the most intimate parts of my private life.... They will remain just that, private.

99

Several hours later, Thomas—his body tense, his voice shaking with emotion—opened the evening session of the hearings with an even stronger statement denying all charges against him. His comments were delivered a few hours after Anita Hill had finished delivering her testimony.

66

I would like to start by saying **unequivocally,** uncategorically that I deny each and every single allegation against me today that suggested in any way that I had conversations of a sexual nature or about pornographic material with Anita Hill, that I ever attempted to date her, that I ever had any personal sexual interest in her, or that I in any way ever harassed her.

Second, and I think a more important point, I think that this today is a **travesty.** I think that it is disgusting. I think that this hearing should never occur in America. This is a case in which this sleaze, this dirt was searched for by staffers of members of this committee, was then leaked to the media, and this committee and this body **validated** it and displayed it in prime time over our entire nation.

How would any member on this committee or any person in this room or any person in this country would like sleaze said about him or her in this fashion or this dirt dredged up and this gossip and these lies displayed in this manner?... The Supreme Court is not worth it. No job is worth it. I am not here for that. I am here for my name, my family, my life and my integrity. I think something is dreadfully wrong with this country, when any person, any person in this free country would be subjected to this....

lynching: an act of mob violence that involves putting someone to death, usually by hanging (meant here in a symbolic sense).

unequivocally: without any doubt whatsoever.

travesty: distorted or inferior imitation of something.

validated: gave official recognition or confirmation to something.

There was an FBI investigation. This is not an opportunity to talk about difficult matters privately or in a closed environment. This is a circus. It is a national disgrace. And from my standpoint, as a black American, as far as I am concerned, it is a high-tech lynching for uppity blacks who in any way **deign** to think for themselves, to do for themselves, to have different ideas, and it is a message that, unless you **kowtow** to an old order, this is what will happen to you, you will be lynched, destroyed, **caricatured** by a committee of the U.S. Senate, rather than hung from a tree.

99

On October 15, 1991, the full Senate voted to confirm Clarence Thomas as an associate justice of the Supreme Court by the narrowest margin in history—fifty-two in favor and forty-eight against. Since then, he has stayed out of the limelight even more than is typical of his fellow justices. Also, he has made few public comments on his nomination process. And as expected, his legal opinions have usually fallen in line with those of Justice Antonin Scalia, by far the most conservative member of the Court.

Sources

Books

Chrisman, Robert, and Robert L. Allen, editors, *Court of Appeal: The Black Community Speaks Out on the Racial and Sexual Politics of Clarence Thomas vs. Anita Hill,* Ballantine, 1992.

Danforth, John C., *The Resurrection: The Confirmation of Clarence Thomas,* Viking, 1994.

Mayer, Jane, and Jill Abramson, *Strange Justice: The Selling of Clarence Thomas,* Houghton, 1994.

Morrison, Toni, editor, *Race-ing Justice, En-Gendering Power: Essays on Anita Hill, Clarence Thomas, and the Construction of Social Reality,* Pantheon, 1992.

Nomination of Judge Clarence Thomas to Be Associate Justice of the Supreme Court of the United States: Hearings Before the Committee on the Judiciary, United States Senate, 102nd Congress, 1st session, Part 4 of 4 parts, October 11, 12, and 13, 1991, pp. 5-10, 157-158, U.S. Government Printing Office, 1993.

deign: reluctantly lower oneself to a less formal or dignified level.

kowtow: show excessive respect out of a sense of inferiority or fear.

caricatured: presented in a totally distorted manner.

Phelps, Timothy M., and Helen Winternitz, *Capitol Games: Clarence Thomas, Anita Hill, and the Story of a Supreme Court Nomination,* Hyperion, 1992.

Simon, Paul, *Advice and Consent: Clarence Thomas, Robert Bork, and the Intriguing History of the Supreme Court's Nomination Battles,* National Press Books, 1992.

Periodicals

Atlantic, "A Question of Fairness," February 1987.

Jet, "Justice Thomas Cast Deciding Vote in Cases That Threatened Affirmative Action," July 3, 1995.

National Review, "Trial by Zeitgeist," January 24, 1994, pp. 48-52.

New Republic, "The Color-Blind Court," July 31, 1995.

Newsweek, "Where Does He Stand?" July 15, 1991, pp. 16-17; "How to Judge a Judge," July 15, 1991, p. 64; "Supreme Mystery," September 16, 1991; "Hearing But Not Speaking," September 16, 1991, p. 23; "Court Charade," September 23, 1991, pp. 18-20; October 28, 1991 (special section covering a variety of topics related to nomination fight); "Who Lied,?" November 14, 1994, pp. 52-54; "Digging for Dirt," November 14, 1994, pp. 55-56.

New York, "Tabloid Government," October 28, 1991, pp. 28-31.

New Yorker, "The Burden of Clarence Thomas," September 27, 1993, pp. 38-51.

New York Times, July 3, 1991; July 16, 1991; "Two Years After His Bruising Hearing, Justice Thomas Can Rarely Be Heard," November 27, 1993, p. 7.

People, "The Making of a Judge," July 22, 1991; "Breaking Silence," November 11, 1991.

Policy Review, "No Room at the Inn: The Loneliness of the Black Conservative," fall, 1991, pp. 72-78.

Time, "Marching to a Different Drummer," July 15, 1991, pp. 18-21; "An Ugly Circus," October 21, 1991; "Truth in the Ruins," October 28, 1991, p. 104; "Judging Thomas," July 13, 1992, pp. 30-31.

U.S. News and World Report, "The Crowning Thomas Affair," September 16, 1991; "Judging Thomas," October 21, 1991, pp. 32-36.

Sojourner Truth

c. 1797–1883

Abolitionist and women's rights activist

Without a doubt, the most famous black female orator of the nineteenth century was Sojourner Truth. Although she never learned to read or write, she was gifted with a certain charisma (a special charm or appeal) that made her especially effective with the spoken word. It was not at all unusual for large crowds to attend her informal talks on slavery and women's rights. And since she believed that God wanted her to share her message with as many people as possible, she traveled and lectured until she was well into her eighties.

Early Life

Sojourner Truth was born a slave named Isabella Baumfree in upstate New York. Bell, as she was known, spent her youth as a member of several different households after she was sold to a new master and separated from her parents at the age of nine. By that time, however, she had already received from her mother a solid moral and spiritual educa-

"THAT MAN OVER THERE SAYS THAT WOMEN NEED TO BE HELPED INTO CARRIAGES, AND LIFTED OVER DITCHES, AND TO HAVE THE BEST PLACE EVERYWHERE. NOBODY EVER HELPS ME INTO CARRIAGES, OR OVER MUD PUDDLES OR GIVES ME ANY BEST PLACE, AND AREN'T I A WOMAN?"

tion. These lessons formed the basis of her lifetime devotion to religion and reform. Truth was sold two more times, ending up in 1810 with a wealthy landowner in New York. There she married an older slave and started a family.

New York State had passed a law requiring all slaveholders to free slaves who were forty years old or older in 1817, and to free all others by 1828. Truth's owner promised to release her a year early, but he did not live up to his word, so she fled with one of her children, an infant daughter. By then, she was separated from her husband and had to find a way to support herself and her family. She was taken in by the Van Wageners, a New York City couple who eventually purchased Truth's freedom for twenty dollars. While staying with the Van Wageners, she learned that her son had illegally been sold out of state. She sued the slaveowner and won, becoming the first black woman to win a lawsuit against a white man.

A New Name and a New Mission

Truth and her two children moved to Manhattan in 1829, where she became involved in a Christian cult formed around Robert Matthews, who claimed to be God the Father. Truth put her life savings into a commune that Matthews formed and worked there as a housekeeper. But when one of the founding members of the group was poisoned after a power struggle in the commune, Truth grew disillusioned and left New York City on June 1, 1843. Only a few miles into her trip, she underwent a profound religious experience during which she heard voices that she believed to be God's. This spiritual reawakening led her to change her name to Sojourner Truth and dedicate herself to a life of urging others to accept Jesus and avoid sin.

*For the next forty years, Truth lived up to her name as the "sojourner," or traveler, ordered to bring enlightenment (insight, especially spiritual) to as many people as possible. She lectured throughout the Northeast and Midwest, broadening her topics to include not only religion but also **abolition**, women's rights, **temperance**, and prison reform. Truth was considered a powerful orator. At nearly six feet tall, with an imposing bearing and a direct gaze, she brought*

abolition: the act of abolishing, or getting rid of, slavery.

temperance: the practice of refusing to drink alcoholic beverages.

skeptical audiences to attention. No matter what subject she addressed, her theme was usually the same, that God is loving, kind, and good, and all human beings should love one another. She was especially skilled at weaving together the idea of freedom for blacks and freedom for women. But her views, unpopular in many circles, also made her the target of abuse and arrest on more than one occasion.

Truth's most famous speech is often known by the title, "Ain't I a Woman?" She delivered it on May 29, 1851, to a women's rights convention in Akron, Ohio. **Presiding** *over the meeting was Frances Gage, who wrote down Truth's remarks in a lower-class southern **dialect** that probably did not reflect her actual speaking style. In fact, she had grown up in the North speaking Dutch and did not even learn English until after she was sold to a new master. And she didn't meet a southerner—white or black—almost until she reached adulthood.*

This first version of Truth's speech originally appeared in Volume 1 of the 1881 book History of Woman Suffrage, *edited by Elizabeth Cady Stanton and others. It appears here with Gage's bracketed notes about the audience's reaction to what Truth was saying. It was later reprinted in* We Shall Be Heard: Women Speakers in America, 1828–Present, *edited by Patricia Scileppi Kennedy and Gloria Hartman O'Shields, Kendall/Hunt, 1983.*

Immediately following the speech as Gage wrote it down is a version without *the southern dialect markers. This is probably more like Truth's actual style of speaking. It was first published in* The Narrative of Sojourner Truth, *an 1878 autobiography by Truth and co-author Olive Gilbert. It was later reprinted in* Man Cannot Speak for Her, Volume 2: Key Texts of the Early Feminists, *by Karlyn Kohrs Campbell, Greenwood Press, 1989.*

❝

[I rose and announced "Sojourner Truth," and begged the audience to keep silence for a few moments. The **tumult** subsided at once, and every eye was fixed on this almost **Amazon** form, which stood nearly six feet high,

presiding: leading.

dialect: a regional variety of a language.

tumult: commotion, noise.

Amazon: a tall, strong, masculine woman.

head erect, and eye piercing the upper air, like one in a dream. At her first word, there was a profound hush. She spoke in deep tones, which, though not loud, reached every ear in the house, and away through the throng at the doors and windows:–]

"Wall, chilern, whar dar is so much racket dar must be somethin' out o' kilter. I tink dat twixt de niggers of de Souf and de woman at de Norf, all talkin' 'bout rights, de white men will be in a fix pretty soon.

"But what's all dis here talkin' 'bout? Dat man ober dar say dat woman needs to be helped into carriages, and lifted ober ditches, and to hab de best place everywhar. Nobody eber helps me into carriages, or ober mud-puddles, or gibs me any best place!" [And raising herself to her full height, and her voice to a pitch like rolling thunder, she asked,] "And ain't I a woman? Look at me! Look at my arm! [and she bared her right arm to the shoulder, showing her tremendous muscular power.] I have ploughed, and planted, and gathered into barns, and no man could head me! And ain't I a woman? I could work as much and eat as much as a man—when I could get it—and bear de lash as well! And ain't I a woman? I have borne thirteen chilern and seen 'em mos' all sold off to slavery, and when I cried out with my mother's grief, none but Jesus heard me! And ain't I a woman?

"Den dey talks 'bout dis ting in de head; what dis dey call it? ["Intellect," whispered some one near.] "Dat's it honey. What's dat got to do wid woman's rights or niggers' rights? If my cup won't hold but a pint, and yourn holds a quart, wouldn't ye be mean not to let me have my little half-measure full?" [And she pointed her significant finger, and sent a keen glance at the minister who had made the argument. The cheering was long and loud.]

"Den dat little man in black dar, he say women can't have as much rights as men, 'cause Christ wan't a woman! Whar did your Christ come from?" [Rolling thunder couldn't have stilled that crowd, as did those deep, wonderful tones, as she stood there with outstretched arms and eyes of fire. Raising her voice still louder, she repeated,] "Whar did your Christ come from? From God and a woman! Man had nothin' to do wid Him." [Oh, what a **rebuke** that was to that little man.]

rebuke: criticism, reprimand.

[Turning again to another objector, she took up the defense of Mother Eve. I can not follow her through it all. It was pointed, and witty, and solemn: eliciting at almost every sentence deafening applause; and she ended by asserting:] "If de fust woman God ever made was strong enough to turn de world upside down all alone, dese women togedder [and she glanced her eye over the platform] ought to be able to turn it back, and get it right side up again! And now dey is asking to do it, de men better let 'em." [Long-continued cheering greeted this.]

"'Bleeged to Ye for hearin' on me, and now ole Sojourner han't got nothin' more to say."

[Amid roars of applause, she returned to her corner, leaving more than one of us with streaming eyes, and hearts beating with gratitude. She had taken us up in her strong arms and carried us safely over the **slough** of difficulty turning the whole tide in our favor. I have never in my life seen anything like the magical influence that subdued the mobbish spirit of the day, and turned the sneers and jeers of an excited crowd into notes of respect and admiration. Hundreds rushed up to shake hands with her, and congratulate the glorious old mother, and bid her God-speed on her mission of "testifyin' agin concerning the wickedness of this 'ere people."]

"

Without any southern dialect markers, the above speech reads as follows:

"

Well, children, where there is so much racket there must be something out o' kilter. I think that 'twixt the Negroes of the South and the women of the North all a-talking about rights, the white men will be in a fix pretty soon.

But what's all this here talking about? That man over there says that women need to be helped into carriages, and lifted over ditches, and to have the best place everywhere. Nobody ever helps me into carriages, or over mud puddles or gives me any best place, and aren't I a woman? Look at me! Look at my arm! I have plowed, and planted, and gathered into barns, and no man could head me—and aren't I a woman? I could work as much and eat as much as a man (when I could get it), and bear the lash as well—and aren't I a woman? I have borne thirteen children and seen them almost all sold

slough: state of spiritual gloom.

off into slavery, and when I cried out with a mother's grief, none but Jesus heard–and aren't I a woman?

Then they talk about this thing in the head–what's this they call it? [Intellect.] That's it honey. What's that got to do with woman's rights or Negroes' rights? If my cup won't hold but a pint and yours holds a quart, wouldn't you be mean not to let me have my little half-measure full?

Then that little man in black there, he says women can't have as much rights as man, 'cause Christ wasn't a woman. Where did your Christ come from? Where did your Christ come from? From God and a woman. Man had nothing to do with him.

If the first woman God ever made was strong enough to turn the world upside down, all alone, these together ought to be able to turn it back and get it right side up again; and now they are asking to do it, the men better let them.

'Bliged to you for hearing on me, and now old Sojourner hasn't got anything more to say.

Truth moved to Battle Creek, Michigan, in 1857. When the Civil War broke out, she nursed Union soldiers and collected contributions of food and clothing for black volunteer regiments. On October 29, 1864, she was received by President Abraham Lincoln at the White House. She remained in Washington for two more years to assist freed slaves, who were then living in refugee camps and slums. In December 1864 the National Freedmen's Relief Association presented her with the title "counsellor to the freed people."

After the Civil War, Truth continued to speak out for women's rights. She was especially concerned that in the drive to obtain voting privileges for newly-freed black men, black women were being ignored. This was a common theme in her lectures at the time.

In May 1867, for example, Truth attended the first annual American Equal Rights Association Convention. Over the course of several days, she delivered a number of speeches in which she again linked the granting of rights to blacks with the granting of rights to women. Her opening address of May 9 set the tone for her later remarks. It is reprinted from Man Cannot Speak for Her, *Volume 2:* Key Texts of the Early Feminists, *by Karlyn Kohrs Campbell, Greenwood Press, 1989.*

❝

My friends, I am rejoiced that you are glad, but I don't know how you will feel when I get through. I come from another field—the country of the slave. They have got their rights—so much good luck: now what is to be done about it? I feel that I have got as much responsibility as anybody else. I have got as good rights as anybody.

There is a great stir about colored men getting their rights, but not a word about the colored women; and if colored men get their rights, and not colored women get theirs, there will be a bad time about it. So I am for keeping the thing going while things are stirring; because if we wait till it is still, it will take a great while to get it going again.

White women are a great deal smarter, and know more than colored women, while colored women do not know scarcely anything. They go out washing, which is about as high as a colored woman gets, and their men go about idle, strutting up and down; and when the women come home, they ask for their money and take it all, and then scold because there is no food. I want you to consider on that, chil'n [sic].

I want women to have their rights. In the courts women have no right, no voice; nobody speaks for them. I wish woman to have her voice there among the **pettifoggers.** If it is not a fit place for women, it is unfit for men to be there.

I am above eighty years old; it is about time for me to be going. But I suppose I am kept here because something remains for me to do; I suppose I am yet to help break the chain.

I have done a great deal of work; as much as a man, but did not get so much pay. I used to work in the field and bind grain, keeping up with the cradler; but men never doing no

pettifoggers: lawyers whose professional conduct and methods are dishonest or immoral.

Sojourner Truth

more, got twice as much pay. So with the German women. They work in the field and do as much work, but do not get the pay. We do as much, we eat as much, we want as much.

I suppose I am about the only colored woman that goes about to speak for the rights of the colored woman. I want to keep the thing stirring, now that the ice is broken. What we want is a little money. You men know that you get as much again as women when you write, or for what you do. When we get our rights, we shall not have to come to you for money, for then we shall have money enough of our own. It is a good consolation to know that when we have got this we shall not be coming to you any more.

You have been having our right so long, that you think, like a slaveholder, that you own us. I know that it is hard for one who has held the reins for so long to give up; it cuts like a knife. It will feel all the better when it closes up again. I have been in Washington about five years, seeing about these colored people. Now colored men have a right to vote; and what I want is to have colored women have the right to vote. There ought to be equal rights more then ever, since colored people have got their freedom.

I am going to talk several times while I am here; so now I will do a little singing. I have not heard any singing since I came here.

[*Accordingly, suiting the action to the word, Sojourner sang, "We are going home."*]

There, children, we shall rest from all our labors; first do all we have to do here.

There I am determined to go, not to stop till I get there to that beautiful place, and I do not mean to stop till I get there.

Sources

Books

Campbell, Karlyn Kohrs, *Man Cannot Speak for Her,* Volume 1: *A Critical Study of Early Feminist Rhetoric,* Volume 2: *Key Texts of the Early Feminists,* Greenwood Press, 1989.

Foner, Philip S., editor, *The Voice of Black America: Major Speeches by Negroes in the United States, 1797–1971,* Simon & Schuster, 1972.

Kennedy, Patricia Scileppi, and Gloria Hartman O'Shields, *We Shall Be Heard: Women Speakers in America, 1828–Present,* Kendall/Hunt, 1983.

Lerner, Gerda, editor, *Black Women in White America: A Documentary History,* Pantheon Books, 1972.

Loewenberg, Bert James, and Ruth Bogin, editors, *Black Women in Nineteenth Century American Life: Their Thoughts, Their Feelings,* Pennsylvania State University Press, 1976.

Mabee, Carlton, and Susan Mabee Newhouse, *Sojourner Truth: Slave, Prophet, Legend,* New York University Press, 1993.

McKissack, Pat, and Fredrick McKissack, *Sojourner Truth: Ain't I a Woman?,* Scholastic, 1992.

Ortiz, Victoria, *Sojourner Truth: A Self-Made Woman,* Lippincott, 1974.

Stanton, Elizabeth Cady, and others, editors, *History of Woman Suffrage,* Volume 1, Fowler & Wells, 1881, reprinted, Arno, 1969.

Truth, Sojourner, and Olive Gilbert, *The Narrative of Sojourner Truth* (reprint of original 1878 edition), Oxford University Press, 1991.

Other

Great American Women's Speeches (sound recording; two cassettes), Caedmon, 1973.

Henry McNeal Turner

1834–1915

Clergyman, politician, and advocate of black nationalism

"THIS IS EITHER A NATION OR A TRAVESTY. IF IT IS A NATION, EVERY MAN EAST AND WEST, NORTH AND SOUTH, IS BOUND TO THE PROTECTION OF HUMAN LIFE AND THE INSTITUTIONS OF THE COUNTRY; BUT IF IT IS A BURLESQUE OR A NATIONAL SHAM, THEN THE WORLD OUGHT TO KNOW IT."

For African Americans, the period between the end of Reconstruction (the reorganization of the Southern states into the Union, which began after the Civil War ended in 1865 and continued until about 1877) through the World War I era (1917–18) was marked by widespread oppression and cruelty that was in some cases worse than anything they had ever experienced under slavery. Lynchings, disenfranchisement (denial of the right to vote), discrimination, segregation, and race riots were commonplace. The U.S. Supreme Court struck down law after law that had guaranteed blacks certain civil rights. Meanwhile, the federal government adopted a "hands-off" policy, especially toward the South.

One of the many voices who challenged this grim state of affairs was Henry McNeal Turner. He was the most outspoken and militant black nationalist (a person who believes that blacks should separate from whites to form their own communities, businesses, and organizations) of his day. In his numerous articles and speeches, he attacked racism and criticized those blacks who hesitated to take radical action against it. As he watched conditions worsen around him, Turner eventually decided on a course of action some considered extreme. He became convinced that only by emigrating (relocating) to Africa could American blacks reclaim their self respect and enjoy basic human rights.

Early Life

A freeborn native of South Carolina, Turner was just a child when his parents bound him to work side-by-side with slaves on local plantations. He escaped that life at the age of fifteen and settled in the town of Abbeville, where he earned a living as a janitor and then as a messenger for a law office. There Turner also learned to read and write, largely through his own efforts. Although he read every book and magazine he could find, he was especially interested in law, medicine, and theology (the study of religious faith and practice).

As a young black man in the South before the Civil War, Turner had few career choices. A desire to enter public life was satisfied in part when he became a traveling evangelist for the Southern Methodist Church. On his tours throughout the southeastern states, he attracted large crowds of whites as well as blacks.

Minister and Politician

While Turner was visiting New Orleans, Louisiana, in 1857 he heard about the black-run African Methodist Episcopal (AME) Church. He immediately joined and then headed to Baltimore, Maryland, to prepare for the ministry. He accepted his first pastorate in 1862 in Washington, D.C. There his flamboyant preaching captured the attention of federal government officials, who appointed him the first black chaplain in the U.S. Army.

After the Civil War ended in 1865, Turner worked briefly for the Freedmen's Bureau in Georgia. (The Freedmen's Bureau was a federal agency, established in 1865 to provide aid and protection to newly freed blacks in the South after the war. One of the most powerful institutions of

Reconstruction, it became a hotbed of debate between the Republican party and Southern Democrats, who forcefully opposed it. The Bureau was officially discontinued in 1869.) He then entered state politics helping to sign up black voters for the Republican party. In early 1868, he served as a delegate to the Georgia state constitutional convention. Later that same year, he was one of twenty-seven African Americans elected as Republicans to the first legislature of Georgia to meet since the end of the war. But white Democrats—who were in the majority—voted to deny them their seats on account of their race. Despite a fiery speech by Turner protesting their decision, the white legislators would not change their minds. This basically shut him out of the world of politics, at least in the South.

Elevated to the Post of Bishop in the AME Church

After serving briefly as postmaster of Macon, Georgia, and as a customs official in Savannah, Georgia, Turner devoted himself to recruiting members for the AME Church. In 1880, he was made a bishop, and for the next thirty-five years he was one of the church's most active and influential leaders.

Over time, Turner grew deeply **disillusioned** by the failure of the United States and its white citizens to make good on their promises to the former slaves. Eventually, he began urging African Americans to emigrate to Africa if they wanted true freedom and equality.

Turner's message appealed to quite a few blacks, especially the "common folk" who rejected the **accommodationist** philosophy of **Booker T. Washington** (see entry) and the **elitism** of **W. E. B. Du Bois** (see entry). But he also ran into strong opposition from some blacks who resented his harsh attacks on those who disagreed with him. Furthermore, transporting emigrants to Africa and establishing a new nation seemed to many to be a pipe dream, since it would have cost more money than any group could raise at the time. Turner nevertheless continued his crusade. From about the mid-1870s until his death in 1915, he was the country's leading **advocate** of black emigration to Africa.

disillusioned: disappointed after becoming aware of being misled.

accommodationist: adapting to the ideas and attitudes of others with an opposing viewpoint.

elitism: the belief that a only a certain superior class of people are fit to serve as a society's leaders.

advocate: promoter, supporter.

*In August 1893 Turner called for a national convention of blacks who supported the idea of seeking radical solutions to the problems they faced. The meeting was held that November in Cincinnati, Ohio. In his opening remarks, Turner explained his concerns and frustrations over the worsening racial situation in the United States. His focus was on **lynching,** which was claiming the lives of an increasing number of black men who were often falsely accused of raping white women. His speech was originally published in the December 1893 issue of Turner's own publication,* Voice of Missions. *An excerpt from it is reprinted here from* Respect Black: The Writings and Speeches of Henry McNeal Turner, *edited by Edwin S. Redkey, Arno, 1971.*

❝

It is known to all present that not a week, and at times scarcely a day, has passed in the last three or four years but what some colored man has been hung, shot or burned by mobs of lynchers, and justified or excused upon the plea that they had outraged some white married or single woman, or some little girl going to or from school. These crimes alleged against us, whether true or false, have been proclaimed by the newspapers of the country in such horrific terms that it would seem like an amazing grace that has held back the curse of God and the vengeance of man, to enable us to meet here today. For if the accusations are even half true, we must be allied to a race of such **incarnate** fiends that no hopeful prospect **illumines** our future.

Now, gentlemen, I shall not presume to affirm or deny the monstrous **imputations,** but certainly as a specific and a race largely regarded as alien by the white people of the country, we owe it to ourselves and posterity to inquire into this subject and give it the most patient, thorough and impartial investigation that ever fell to the lot of man. If the charges are true, then God has no attribute that will side with us. Nature has no member, no potential factor, that will defend us.... Nor can we excuse it, **palliate** it or **manifest** indifference upon the **postulation** that it is a **righteous retribution** upon the white man for the way he treated our women for hundreds of years. For if the countercharge is

lynching: an act of mob violence that involves putting someone to death, usually by hanging.

incarnate: given physical (especially human) form and nature.

illumines: makes shine or light up.

imputations: accusations.

palliate: downplay, or make excuses for.

manifest: show.

postulation: claim, theory.

righteous retribution: morally excusable punishment.

true, we certainly did not visit swift vengeance upon the white man, as he is doing upon us by his lawless mobs.

There is but one recourse left us that will command the respect of the civilized world and the approval of God, and that is to investigate the facts in the premises, and if guilty, acknowledge it, and let us organize against the wretches in our own ranks.... Let us do everything within the bounds of human endeavor to arrest this flood tide of vice and redeem the good name which we have borne through all the ages, for the protection of female honor....

But, gentlemen of the convention, there is another side to this question. Under the genius and theory of civilization throughout the world, no man is guilty of any crime, whatever, until he is arrested, tried by an impartial process of law and deliberately convicted.... Lynching a man is an act of barbarism and cannot be justified by even what a distinguished bishop terms "emotional insanity." For even insanity has no authority to intrude its maddened vengeance upon the law and order of the public.

Judge O'Neil, of South Carolina, many years ago, long before freedom was contemplated, sentenced two white men to the gallows for putting a slave Negro to death without legal process, and they were hung dead by the neck.... This, too, was at a time when the theory prevailed that black men, especially slaves, had no rights that white men were bound to respect. But now, a quarter of a century after we are free, a mob can band themselves together and hang a Negro about perpetrating a rape upon some white woman, but rarely give the name of the individual, and when you visit the community and inquire as to who it was thus outraged, in many instances, nobody knows, and the mob is justified upon the plea that the Negro confessed it. Confessed it to whom? Confessed it to a set of bloody-handed murderers, just as though a set of men who were cruel enough to take the life of another were too moral to tell a lie. Strange, too, that the men who constitute these **banditti** can never be identified by the respective governors or the law officers, but the newspapers know all about them....

I fear that what I have been told in confidence by prominent white men, that a large number of associations are in

banditti: outlaws.

existence, bound by solemn oaths and pledged to secrecy by the most binding **covenants,** to exterminate the Negro by utilizing every possible opportunity, has more truth in it than I was at first inclined to believe. For the white people all over the country have everything in their own hands, can do absolutely as they please in administering their own created laws to the Negro. They have all the judges, and all the juries, and virtually all the lawyers, all the jails, all the penitentiaries, all the ropes, all the powder, and all the guns.... Why these hasty, illegal executions unless Negro extermination is the object desired? They evidently must fear a public trial, otherwise it is very **singular** that they should be so anxious to silence the tongue and close the lips of the only one who can speak in his own defense by putting him to death so hastily and without judge or jury.

The white people of this country, almost without exception, claim to be constitutionally superior to the black man. Then why should a race so superior and so numerically, financially, and intellectually in advance of the colored man be so afraid of a raping wretch that they will not allow him a chance to open his inferior lips in his own defense? Gentlemen, it is a serious question, and this council must consider and pass upon both of these grave issues—the black rapers on the one hand, and the exterminators of the blacks on the other.

I know it is held that if you give a Negro who is charged with outraging a white woman a fair trial, that the process of the law will be so long, tedious and so many technicalities are liable to be raised, that the time and expense would be worth more than the life of the victim. But rather than flood the land with blood, especially if it should be innocent blood, and the **retributive** vengeance of an angry God, we had far better ask for the old slave time trial before a justice of the peace, and abide by its consequences, for such as are accused of this revolting crime, or, vulgar and shocking as it would be, do the next best thing, and the thing that will effectually cure this evil, if you should find that it actually exists. Let the raper be castrated and let him live and remain as a monument of his folly and madness. Certainly he will never repeat the crime, and it would be far better than shedding so much of what may be innocent blood.....

covenants: agreements.
singular: odd.
retributive: given as punishment.

Let us ask Congress for a law to banish them from the country. Thousands of white criminals were banished from England over here, all through the seventeenth century, and many of the offspring of these banished criminals are the lynchers of today. If Rome, Scotland and England could banish their irredeemable white criminals, surely this country can banish its black criminals. But spare the lives of the wretches. For there is but one deed that God permits the taking of human life for, anyway, and that is for the crime of murder. Horrible as the crime of raping may be, it is a grave question whether it merits the death penalty or not. I do not believe it does when there are so many other ways he can be adequately punished, unless the perpetration of the satanic deed involves the death of the outraged....

Unless this nation, North and South, East and West, awakes from its slumbers and calls a halt to the reign of blood and carnage in this land, its dissolution and utter extermination is only a question of a short time. For Egypt went down; Greece went down; Babylon went down; Nineveh went down; Rome went down, and other nations numerically stronger than the United States, and the spirit of conquest, cruelty, injustice and domination was the death of them all and the United States will never celebrate another centennial of undivided states, without a change of programme.

A Negro is a very small item in the body politic of this country, but his groans, prayers and innocent blood will speak to God day and night, and the God of the poor and helpless will come to his relief sooner or later, and another **fratricidal** war will be the sequence, though it may grow out of an issue as far from the Negro as midday is from midnight. For this is either a nation or a **travesty.** If it is a nation, every man East and West, North and South, is bound to the protection of human life and the institutions of the country; but if it is a **burlesque** or a national sham, then the world ought to know it. The North is responsible for every outrage perpetrated in the South, and the South is responsible for every outrage perpetrated in the North, and so of the East and West, and it is no use to blame the South and excuse the North, or blame the North and excuse the South. For any species of injustice perpetrated upon the Negro, every man in every portion of this nation, if it is a nation, is responsible.

fratricidal: brother against brother, in this case the states against each other.

travesty: distorted or inferior imitation.

burlesque: farce.

Henry McNeal Turner

The truth is, the nation as such, has no disposition to give us manhood protection anyway. Congress had constitutional power to pursue a runaway slave by legislation into any state and punish the man who would dare conceal him, and the Supreme Court of the United States sustained its legislation as long as slavery existed. Now the same Supreme Court has the power to declare that the Negro has no civil rights under the general government that will protect his citizenship, and authorize the states to legislate upon and for us, as they may like; and they are passing special acts to degrade the Negro by authority of the said high tribunal, and Congress proposes no remedy by legislation or by such a constitutional amendment as will give us the status of citizenship in the nation that is presumed we are to love and to sacrifice our lives, if need be, in the defense of.

Yet Congress can legislate for the protection of the fish in the sea and the seals that **gambol** in our waters, and obligate its mien, its money, its navy, its army and its flag to protect, but the eight million or ten million of its black men and women ... must be turned off to become the prey of violence, and when we appeal to the general government for protection and recognition, Justice, so-called, drops her scales and says, away with you.

I am abused as no other man in this nation because I am an African emigrationist, and while we are not here assembled to consider that question, nor do I mention it at the present time to impose it upon you, but if the present condition of things is to continue, I had not only rather see my people in the heart of Africa, but in ice-bound, ice-covered and ice-fettered Greenland. "Give me liberty or give me death!"

,,

Sources

Books

Aptheker, Herbert, editor, *A Documentary History of the Negro People in the United States,* Volume 2: *From the Reconstruction Years to the Founding of the NAACP in 1910,* Citadel, 1964.

gambol: play, frolic.

Bracey, John H., Jr., August Meier, and Elliott Rudwick, editors, *Black Nationalism in America,* Bobbs-Merrill, 1970.

Foner, Philip S., *The Voice of Black America: Major Speeches by Negroes in the United States, 1797-1971,* Simon & Schuster, 1972.

Redkey, Edwin S., *Black Exodus: Black Nationalist and Back-to-Africa Movements, 1890-1910,* Yale University Press, 1969.

Redkey, Edwin S., editor, *Respect Black: The Writings and Speeches of Henry McNeal Turner,* Arno, 1971.

Periodicals

Journal of American History, "Bishop Turner's African Dream," September 1967, pp. 271-290.

Booker T. Washington

1856-1915

Educator and statesman

Early Life

Booker T. Washington was born into slavery on a plantation in Hale's Ford, Virginia, around April 5, 1856. (No one kept records of the exact date.) His father was an unknown white man, and his mother was the plantation's cook, a woman named Jane. Soon after Booker was born, Jane married a fellow slave, Washington Ferguson. He ran away to Malden, West Virginia, during the Civil War, and it was not until after the war ended in 1865 that the rest of his family joined him there.

At his stepfather's insistence, Booker went to work at the age of nine. His first jobs were in the local salt and coal mines. Later, he served as a houseboy for a woman named Mrs. Ruffner, whose husband owned the mines. Mrs. Ruffner was very strict and proper lady from New England who valued cleanliness, order, and good work habits. She made a strong impression on her young employee, who gained a lifelong appreciation for what he had learned in the Ruffner home.

"THE WISEST AMONG MY RACE UNDERSTAND THAT THE AGITATION OF QUESTIONS OF SOCIAL EQUALITY IS THE EXTREMIST FOLLY, AND THAT PROGRESS IN THE ENJOYMENT OF ALL THE PRIVILEGES THAT WILL COME TO US MUST BE THE RESULT OF SEVERE AND CONSTANT STRUGGLE RATHER THAN OF ARTIFICIAL FORCING."

Washington attended school whenever he could, which wasn't very often. Much of what he learned was through his own readings and studies. At sixteen, he set out to fulfill his dream of going to college. Traveling mostly on foot and with almost no money, he made his way to Hampton, Virginia. There he was accepted into the Hampton Institute, a well-known vocational school for blacks that stressed training in practical skills and the importance of having high moral standards. Washington worked as a janitor to help pay for his education and graduated with honors in 1875.

Establishes Tuskegee Institute

In 1881, when he was only twenty-five, Washington was hired to establish and head a school similar to the Hampton Institute in Tuskegee, Alabama. When the ambitious young educator arrived in Tuskegee to start his new job, he discovered that state government officials had not even bought any land, put up any buildings, or hired any staff. So Washington immediately launched a one-man effort to raise funds, recruit students and teachers, and develop classes and programs. He was so successful that in less than ten years the Tuskegee Institute had won national acclaim for its emphasis on achieving black economic advancement through self-help programs. And as Tuskegee became more and more famous, Washington found himself well on his way to becoming one of the best known and most respected black men in America.

On September 18, 1895, Washington gave one of the opening speeches at the Cotton States and International Exposition in Atlanta, Georgia. His talk before the racially-mixed audience focused on his belief that it was time for African Americans to put aside their desire for civil and social equality. Instead, he advised blacks to concentrate on making themselves a vital part of the nation's economy through education and work. Once blacks had demonstrated their ability to be productive citizens, he said, whites would most certainly grant them the rights that years of protests had not yet won.

The audience greeted Washington with polite applause when he was first introduced. But after delivering his fifteen-

*minute address—which came to be known as the "Atlanta Compromise" speech—the Tuskegee president left the stage to the sound of a thunderous ovation. Washington's ideas quickly gained the enthusiastic support of whites and many blacks throughout the country. For the next twenty years, he was the foremost spokesman for black America. But more militant African Americans such as **W. E. B. Du Bois** (see entry) scorned Washington and his "compromise" as foolish and self-defeating. They did not believe that whites would ever willingly grant blacks equality without a struggle.*

The text of Washington's speech originally appeared in his autobiography, Up from Slavery. *The following version is reprinted from* The Negro Almanac, *Gale, 1989.*

❝

Mr. President and Gentlemen of the Board of Directors and Citizens:

One-third of the population of the South is of the Negro race. No enterprise seeking the material, civil, or moral welfare of this section can disregard this element of our population and reach the highest success. I but convey to you, Mr. President and Directors, the sentiment of the masses of my race when I say that in no way have the value and manhood of the American Negro been more fittingly and generously recognized than by the managers of this magnificent Exposition at every stage of its progress. It is a recognition that will do more to cement the friendship of the two races than any occurrence since the dawn of our freedom.

Not only this, but the opportunity here afforded will awaken among us a new era of industrial progress. Ignorant and inexperienced, it is not strange that in the first years of our new life we began at the top instead of at the bottom; that a seat in Congress or the State Legislature was more sought than real estate or industrial skill; that the political convention or stump speaking had more attractions than starting a dairy farm or a truck garden.

A ship lost at sea for many days suddenly sighted a friendly vessel. From the mast of the unfortunate vessel was seen a signal: "Water, water; we die of thirst!" The answer from the friendly vessel at once came back: "Cast down your bucket where you are." A second time the signal, "Water, water; send us water!" ran up from the distressed vessel, and was answered, "Cast down your bucket where you are." And a third and fourth signal for water was answered: "Cast down your bucket where you are." The captain of the distressed vessel, at last heeding the injunction, cast down his bucket, and it came up full of fresh, sparkling water from the mouth of the Amazon River. To those of my race who depend on bettering their condition in a foreign land, or who underestimate the importance of cultivating friendly relations with the Southern white man, who is their next door neighbor, I would say: "Cast down your bucket where you are"—cast it down in making friends in every manly way of the people of all races by whom we are surrounded.

Cast it down in agriculture, mechanics, in commerce, in domestic service, and in the professions. And in this connection it is well to bear in mind that whatever other sins the South may be called to bear, when it comes to business, pure and simple, it is in the South that the Negro is given a man's chance in the commercial world, and in nothing is this Exposition more eloquent than in emphasizing this chance. Our greatest danger is, that in the great leap from slavery to freedom we may overlook the fact that the masses of us are to live by the production of our hands, and fail to keep in mind that we shall prosper in proportion as we learn to dignify and glorify common labor, and put brains and skill into the common occupations of life; shall prosper in proportion as we learn to draw the line between the superficial and the substantial, the ornamental **gewgaws** of life and the useful. No race can prosper till it learns that there is as much dignity in tilling a field as in writing a poem. It is at the bottom of life we must begin, and not at the top. Nor should we permit our grievances to overshadow our opportunities.

To those of the white race who look to the incoming of those of foreign birth and strange tongue and habits for the prosperity of the South, were I permitted, I would repeat what I say to my own race, "Cast down your bucket where you are." Cast it down among the 8,000,000 Negroes whose habits you know, whose fidelity and love you have tested in days when to have proved treacherous meant the ruin of

gewgaws: trinkets.

Washington at work: "There is no defense or security for any of us except in the highest intelligence and development of all."

your firesides. Cast down your bucket among these people who have, without strikes or labor wars, tilled your fields, cleared your forests, builded your railroads and cities, and brought forth treasures from the bowels of the earth, and helped make possible this magnificent representation of the progress of the South. Casting down your bucket among my people, helping and encouraging them as you are doing on these grounds, and, with education of head, hand and heart, you will find that they will buy your surplus land, make blossom the waste place in your fields, and run your factories. While doing this, you can be sure in the future, as in the past, that you and your families will be surrounded by the most patient, faithful, law-abiding, and unresentful people that the world has seen. As we have proved our loyalty to

Historically Black Colleges and Universities

Tuskegee Institute was one of many colleges founded after the Civil War for the purpose of providing education to former slaves. Until traditionally white colleges and universities began accepting black students in greater numbers in the 1950s and especially the 1960s, most African Americans who wanted to obtain more than just a basic education attended a historically black college. A few of these institutions—such as Pennsylvania's Lincoln University—had been established before the Civil War in a couple of northern states. But it was not until after the Civil War that the vast majority of black colleges sprang up in southern states.

For nearly a hundred years, places like Howard University, Atlanta University in Georgia, and Tennessee's Fisk University were among the only schools that provided college-level studies to blacks who had been shut out of white colleges and universities. Now many blacks attend formerly segregated schools, resulting in decreasing enrollments at a number of historically black colleges and universities. This has led some people to question whether there is still a need for all-black institutions in a country that is supposedly committed to the idea of integration. Others argue, however, that historically black colleges and universities offer a type of support and a nurturing environment that African American students cannot usually find elsewhere.

you in the past, in nursing your children, watching by the sick bed of your mothers and fathers, and often following them with tear-dimmed eyes to their graves, so in the future, in our humble way, we shall stand by you with a devotion that no foreigner can approach, ready to lay down our lives, if need be, in defense of yours, interlacing our industrial, commercial, civil, and religious life with yours in a way that shall make the interests of both races one. In all things that are purely social we can be as separate as the fingers, yet one as the hand in all things essential to mutual progress.

There is no defense or security for any of us except in the highest intelligence and development of all. If anywhere there are efforts tending to curtail the fullest growth of the Negro, let these efforts be turned into stimulating, encouraging, and making him the most useful and intelligent citizen. Effort or means so invested will pay a thousand percent interest. These efforts will be twice blessed—"blessing him that gives and him that takes."

There is no escape through law of man or God from the inevitable:

The laws of changeless justice bind
Oppressor with oppressed;
As close as sin and suffering joined
We march to fate abreast.

Nearly sixteen millions of hands will aid you in pulling the load upwards, or they will pull against you the load downwards. We shall constitute one-third and more of the ignorance and crime of the South, or one-third its intelligence and progress; we shall contribute one-third to the business and industrial prosperity of the South, or we shall prove a veritable body of death, stagnating, depressing, retarding every effort to advance the body politic.

Gentlemen of the Exposition, as we present to you our humble effort at an exhibition of our progress, you must not expect over much. Starting thirty years ago with ownership here and there in a few quilts and pumpkins and chickens (gathered from miscellaneous sources), remember the path that has led from these to the invention and production of agricultural implements, buggies, steam engines, newspapers, books, statuary, carving, paintings, the management of drug stores and banks, has not been trodden without contact with thorns and thistles. While we take pride in what we exhibit as a result of our independent efforts, we do not for a moment forget that our part in this exhibition would fall far short of your expectations but for the constant help that has come to our educational life, not only from the Southern states, but especially from Northern **philanthropists,** who have made their gifts a constant stream of blessing and encouragement.

The wisest among my race understand that the agitation of questions of social equality is the extremist folly, and that progress in the enjoyment of all the privileges that will come to us must be the result of severe and constant struggle rather than of artificial forcing. No race that has anything to contribute to the markets of the world is long in any degree **ostracized.** It is important and right that all privileges of the law be ours, but it is vastly more important that we be prepared for the exercise of those privileges. The opportunity to earn a dollar in a factory just now is worth infinitely more than the opportunity to spend a dollar in an opera house.

In conclusion, may I repeat that nothing in thirty years

philanthropists: people who donate money or other kinds of support toward humanitarian efforts.

ostracized: excluded, shut out.

A classroom at Tuskegee Institute, Alabama, founded by Washington in 1881

has given us more hope and encouragement, and drawn us so near to you of the white race, as this opportunity offered by the Exposition; and here bending, as it were, over the altar that represents the results of the struggles of your race and mine, both starting practically empty-handed three decades ago, I pledge that, in your effort to work out the great and intricate problem which God has laid at the doors of the South, you shall have at all time the patient, sympathetic help of my race; only let this be constantly in mind that, while from representations in these buildings of the product of field, of forest, of mine, of factory, letters, and art, much good will come, yet far above and beyond material benefits will be that higher good, that let us pray God will come, in a blotting out of sectional differences and racial **animosities** and suspicions, in a determination to administer absolute justice, in a willing obedience among all classes to the mandates of law. This, coupled with our material prosperity, will bring into our beloved South a new heaven and a new earth.

,,

animosities: hatreds.

Washington remained influential among white Americans until his death on November 14, 1915. But he had lost a great deal of his power and prestige among African Americans by then, especially among younger and more liberal blacks who had begun to look elsewhere for leadership. They often turned to people associated with more militant groups such as the newly-formed National Association for the Advancement of Colored People (NAACP), whose leaders had strongly criticized Washington and his policies over the years. In fact, some held him partly responsible for making relations between blacks and whites worse instead of better during the early 1900s because he tolerated the increasing racial oppression of African Americans.

Sources

Books

Boulware, Marcus Hanna, *The Oratory of Negro Leaders: 1900–1968,* Negro Universities Press, 1969.

Foner, Philip S., editor, *The Voice of Black America: Major Speeches by Negroes in the United States, 1797–1971,* Simon & Schuster, 1972.

Harlan, Louis R., *Booker T. Washington: The Making of a Black Leader, 1856–1901,* Oxford University Press, 1972.

Harlan, Louis R., and others, editors, *The Booker T. Washington Papers,* fourteen volumes, University of Illinois Press, 1972–1989.

Hill, Roy L., *Rhetoric of Racial Revolt,* Golden Bell Press, 1964.

Meier, August, *Negro Thought in America, 1880–1915: Racial Ideologies in the Age of Booker T. Washington,* University of Michigan Press, 1963.

Meltzer, Milton, editor, *The Black Americans: A History in Their Own Words, 1619–1983,* Crowell, 1984.

Ploski, Harry A., and James Williams, editors, *The Negro Almanac: A Reference Work on the African American,* fifth edition, Gale, 1989.

Schroeder, Alan, *Booker T. Washington,* Chelsea House, 1992.

Smith, Arthur L., and Stephen Robb, editors, *The Voice of Black Rhetoric: Selections,* Allyn & Bacon, 1971.

Thornbrough, Emma Lou, editor, *Booker T. Washington,* Prentice-Hall, 1969.

Washington, Booker T., *The Story of My Life and Work* (reprint), Greenwood Press, 1970.

Washington, Booker T., *Up from Slavery* (reprint), Viking Penguin, 1986.

Washington, Booker, T., *My Larger Education* (reprint), Mnemosyne Publishing, 1969.

Periodicals

Ebony, "Ten Greats of Black History," August 1972, pp. 35–42.

New York Times (obituary), November 15, 1915.

Ida B. Wells-Barnett

1862–1930

Journalist and anti-lynching activist

During the late nineteenth and early twentieth century, Ida B. Wells-Barnett launched and headed a one-woman crusade against the vicious crime of lynching. Lynching is an act of mob violence that involves putting someone to death, usually by hanging. In the decade from 1890 to 1900 alone, lynching claimed more than 1,200 black lives (mostly men, but also some women and children), and had become a widespread—and even to some extent an accepted—practice in the South. Mobs generally justified lynching as a means of punishing crimes, but they did not give their victims the benefit of a trial. One of the more common accusations made against black male lynching victims was that they had raped a white woman, but in many instances the people who were lynched had clearly committed no violent crime. Wells-Barnett showed, rather, that the victims had frequently been involved in intimate relations with white women, to which these women had fully consented. The federal government did little or noth-

"THERE IS LITTLE DIFFERENCE BETWEEN THE ANTEBELLUM SOUTH AND THE NEW SOUTH. HER WHITE CITIZENS ARE WEDDED TO ANY METHOD HOWEVER REVOLTING, ANY MEASURE HOWEVER EXTREME, FOR THE SUBJUGATION OF THE YOUNG MANHOOD OF THE RACE."

ing to prevent the killings, claiming that law enforcement was the role of individual states.

To Wells-Barnett, lynching was nothing more than a deadly form of racial prejudice. No decent human being, she argued, could possibly ignore it or justify it. She waged her war against lynching in the press and on the speaker's platform despite numerous efforts to intimidate her into abandoning the fight. In the process, she earned a reputation for fearlessness and determination

Early Life

Wells-Barnett was born into slavery in Holly Springs, Mississippi. Following the Civil War and emancipation, she attended a high school and industrial college established by Methodist missionaries from the North. When Wells-Barnett was about sixteen, however, her parents died in a yellow fever epidemic. She then went to work as a teacher to support herself and her five younger brothers and sisters.

In 1884, Wells-Barnett moved to Memphis, Tennessee, and taught there for several years. She also began writing for various local black newspapers as well as some national publications. In 1889 she became part owner and editor of the Free Speech *newspaper in Memphis. In the pages of that newspaper her angry condemnation of lynching began to attract attention throughout the United States and even overseas.*

Urges Blacks to Protest Against Lynching

In 1892, Wells-Barnett herself became the target of death threats. After three black grocers were kidnapped and brutally murdered, she published a series of scathing editorials urging blacks to boycott the city's new streetcar line and move out of Memphis if at all possible. Furious whites responded by burning the offices of the Free Speech. *Realizing it was too dangerous for her to remain in town, she moved to New York City. There she continued her crusade as a columnist for the nation's leading black newspaper, the* New York Age. *In addition, Wells-Barnett began giving lectures throughout the North and in Europe and Great Britain. She later settled in Chicago and was a found-*

*ing member, along with **W. E. B. Du Bois** (see entry) and other African American activists, of both the Niagara Movement and the National Association for the Advancement of Colored People (NAACP). The Niagara Movement was formed in 1905 with the purpose of ending racial discrimination and achieving social and political equality for blacks. It became known as the NAACP in 1910 and its major function for many years to come was to fight the lynching of black people throughout the United States.*

*In February 1893, **Frederick Douglass** (see entry) invited Wells-Barnett to Washington, D.C., to talk about her anti-lynching campaign at the Metropolitan African Methodist Episcopal Church. She had recently published a booklet entitled* Southern Horrors *in which she examined the circumstances surrounding various lynchings and challenged the widely-held belief that lynchers were only trying to protect white women from being raped by black men. Like many of her fellow African Americans, Wells-Barnett believed that if northern whites knew how extensive the slaughter of innocent black men was in the South, they would take steps to put an end to it. An excerpt from her long speech follows. It is reprinted from* Man Cannot Speak for Her, *Volume 2:* Key Texts of the Early Feminists, *by Karlyn Kohrs Campbell, Greenwood Press, 1989.*

❝

Wednesday evening, May 24, 1892, the city of Memphis was filled with excitement. Editorials in the daily papers of that date caused a meeting to be held in the Cotton Exchange Building; a committee was sent for the editors of the *Free Speech,* an Afro-American journal published in that city, and the only reason the open threats of lynching that were made were not carried out was because they could not be found. The cause of all this commotion was the following editorial published in the *Free Speech* May 21, 1892, the Saturday previous.

Eight Negroes lynched since last issue of the *Free Speech,* one at Little Rock, Arkansas, last Saturday morning where the citizens broke (?) into the penitentiary and got their man; three near Anniston, Alabama, one near New Orleans; and three at Clarksville, Georgia, the last three for killing a white man, and five on the same old racket—the new alarm about raping white women. The same programme of hanging, then shooting bullets into the lifeless bodies was carried out to the letter.

Nobody in this section of the country believes the old threadbare lie that Negro men rape white women. If Southern white men are not careful, they will over-reach themselves and public sentiment will have a reaction; a conclusion will then be reached which will be very damaging to the moral reputation of their women.

The *Daily Commercial* [a white newspaper] of Wednesday following, May 25, contained the following leader:

Those negroes who are attempting to make the lynching of individuals of their race a means for arousing the worst passions of their kind are playing with a dangerous sentiment. The negroes may as well understand that there is no mercy for the negro rapist and little patience with his defenders. A negro organ [the *Free Speech*] printed in this city, in a recent issue publishes the following atrocious paragraph: "Nobody in this section of the country believes the old thread-bare lie that Negro men rape white women. If Southern white men are not careful they will over-reach themselves, and public sentiment will have a reaction; and a conclusion will be reached which will be very damaging to the moral reputation of their women."

The fact that a black scoundrel is allowed to live and utter such loathsome and repulsive **calumnies** is a volume of evidence as to the wonderful patience of Southern whites. But we have had enough of it.

There are some things that the Southern white man will not tolerate, and the obscene intimations of the foregoing have brought the writer to the very outermost limit of public patience. We hope we have said enough.

The *Evening Scimitar* [another white newspaper] of same date, copied the *Commercial*'s editorial with these words of comment:

Patience under such circumstances is not a virtue. If the negroes themselves do not apply the remedy without delay it will be the duty of those whom he has attacked to tie the

calumnies: false charges.

Wells-Barnett: "I feel that the race and the public generally should have a statement of the facts as they exist."

wretch who utters these calumnies to a stake at the intersection of Main and Madison Streets, brand him in the forehead with a hot iron and perform upon him a surgical operation with a pair of tailor's shears.

Acting upon this advice, the leading citizens met in the Cotton Exchange Building the same evening, and threats of lynching were freely indulged, not by the lawless element upon which the deviltry of the South is usually saddled—but by the leading business men, in their leading business center. Mr. Fleming, the business manager and owning a half interest [in] the *Free Speech,* had to leave town to escape the mob, and was afterwards ordered not to return; letters and telegrams sent me in New York where I was spending my vacation advised me that bodily harm awaited my return. Creditors took possession of the office and sold the outfit, and the *Free Speech* was as if it had never been.

The editorial in question was prompted by the many inhuman and fiendish lynchings of Afro-Americans which have recently taken place and was meant as a warning. Eight lynched in one week and five of them charged with rape! The thinking public will not easily believe freedom and education more brutalizing than slavery, and the world knows that the crime of rape was unknown during four years of civil war, when the white women of the South were at the mercy of the race which is all at once charged with being a **bestial** one.

Since my business has been destroyed and I am an exile from home because of that editorial, the issue has been forced, and as the writer of it I feel that the race and the public generally should have a statement of the facts as they exist. They will serve at the same time as a defense for the Afro-American Sampsons [sic] who suffer themselves to be betrayed by white Delilahs.

The whites of Montgomery, Alabama, knew J. C. Duke sounded the keynote of the situation—which they would gladly hide from the world, when he said in his paper, the *Herald,* five years ago: "Why is it that white women attract negro men now more than in former days? There was a time when such a thing was unheard of. There is a secret to this thing, and we greatly suspect it is the growing appreciation of white Juliets for colored Romeos." Mr. Duke, like the *Free Speech* proprietors, was forced to leave the city for reflecting on the "honah" of white women and his paper suppressed; but the truth remains that Afro-American men do not always rape (?) white women without their consent.

Mr. Duke, before leaving Montgomery, signed a card disclaiming any intention of **slandering** Southern white women. The editor of the *Free Speech* has no disclaimer to

bestial: savage, barbaric.

slandering: making statements intended to damage someone's reputation.

enter, but asserts instead that there are many white women in the South who would marry colored men if such an act would not place them at once beyond the pale of society and within the clutches of the law. The **misceg[e]nation** laws of the South only operate against the legitimate union of the races; they leave the white man free to seduce all the colored girls he can, but it is death to the colored man who yields to the force and advances of a similar attraction in white women. White men lynch the offending Afro-American, not because he is a despoiler of virtue, but because he succumbs to the smiles of white women....

[Wells-Barnett then summarized a story that had appeared in the Cleveland Gazette *newspaper about a married white woman in the Ohio town of Elyria who accused a black man of rape to cover up the fact that they had really been lovers.]*

There are thousands of such cases throughout the South, with the difference that the Southern white men in **insatiate** fury wreak their vengeance without intervention of law upon the Afro-Americans who **consort** with their women. A few instances to substantiate the assertion that some white women love the company of the Afro-American will not be out of place. Most of these cases were reported by the daily papers of the South.

[At this point, Wells-Barnett gave more than a half dozen examples of white women who had shocked and angered fellow whites by living with and sometimes having children by black men. In most cases, the women left town on their own or were sent away in disgrace. The men were forced to flee for their lives; some did not manage to get away and were lynched.]

These are not pleasant facts, but they are illustrative of the vital phase of the so-called "race question," which should properly be designated an earnest inquiry as to the best methods by which religion, science, law and political power may be employed to excuse injustice, barbarity and crime done to a people because of race and color. There can be no possible belief that these people were inspired by any consuming zeal to vindicate God's law against misceg[e]nationists of the most practical sort. The woman was a willing part-

miscegenation: mixing of the white race with other races through marriage.

insatiate: incapable of being satisfied.

consort: associate, socialize.

ner in the victim's guilt, and being of the "superior" race must naturally have been more guilty....

Hundreds of such cases might be cited, but enough have been given to prove the assertion that there are white women in the South who love the Afro-American's company even as there are white men notorious for their preference for Afro-American women.

There is hardly a town in the South which has not an instance of the kind which is well known, and hence the assertion is **reiterated** that "nobody in the South believes the old thread-bare lie that Negro men rape white women." Hence there is a growing demand among Afro-Americans that the guilt or innocence of parties accused of rape be fully established. They know the men of the section of the country who refuse this are not so desirous of punishing rapists as they pretend. The utterances of the leading white men show that with them it is not the crime but the class. Bishop Fitzgerald has become apologist for lynchers of the rapists of white women only. Governor Tillman, of South Carolina, in the month of June, standing under the tree in Barnwell, South Carolina, on which eight Afro-Americans were hung last year, declared that he would "lead a mob to lynch a negro who raped a white woman." So say the pulpits, officials and newspapers of the South. But when the victim is a colored woman it is different.....

[Wells-Barnett then described several cases in which white men were not punished for raping black girls and women.]

The appeal of Southern whites to Northern sympathy and sanction, the **adroit, insid[i]ous** plea made by Bishop Fitzgerald for suspension of judgment because those "who condemn lynching express no sympathy for the white woman in the case," falls to the ground in the light of the foregoing.

From this exposition of the race issue in lynch law, the whole matter is explained by the well-known opposition growing out of slavery to the progress of the race. This is crystalized in the oft-repeated slogan: "This is a white man's country and the white man must rule." The South resented giving the Afro-American his freedom, the ballot box, and

reiterated: repeated.

adroit: clever.

insidious: subtle and potentially harmful.

the Civil Rights Law. The raids of the Ku-Klux and White Liners to subvert reconstruction government, the Hamburg and Ellerton, South Carolina, the Copiah County, Mississippi, and the Lafayette Parish, Louisiana, massacres were excused as the natural resentment of intelligence against government by ignorance.

Honest white men practically conceded the necessity of intelligence murdering ignorance to correct the mistake of the general government, and the race was left to the tender mercies of the solid South. Thoughtful Afro-Americans with the strong arm of the government withdrawn and with the hope to stop such wholesale massacres urged the race to sacrifice its political rights for the sake of peace. They honestly believed the race should fit itself for government, and when that should be done, the objection to race participation in politics would be removed.

But the sacrifice did not remove the trouble, nor move the South to justice. One by one the Southern States have legally (?) **disfranchised** the Afro-American, and since the repeal of the Civil Rights Bill nearly every Southern state has passed separate car laws with a penalty against their infringement. The race regardless of advancement is penned into filthy, stifling partitions cut off from smoking cars. All this while, although the political cause has been removed, the butcheries of black men at Barnwell, South Carolina, Carrolton, Mississippi, Waycross, Georgia, and Memphis, Tennessee, have gone on; also the **flaying** alive of a man in Kentucky, the burning of one in Arkansas, the hanging of a fifteen-year-old girl in Louisiana, a woman in Jackson, Tennessee, and one in Hollendale, Mississippi, until the dark and bloody record of the South shows 728 Afro-Americans lynched during the past 8 years. Not 50 of these were for political causes; the rest were for all manner of accusations from that of rape of white women, to the case of the boy Will Lewis who was hanged at Tullahoma, Tennessee, last year for being drunk and "sassy" to white folks.

These statistics, compiled by the Chicago *Tribune*, were given the first of this year (1892). Since then, not less than one hundred and fifty have been known to have met violent death at the hands of cruel bloodthirsty mobs during the past nine months.

disfranchised: denied the right to vote to.

flaying: stripping the skin off of something.

To **palliate** this record (which grows worse as the Afro-American becomes intelligent) and excuse some of the most heinous crimes that ever stained the history of a country, the South is shielding itself behind the plausible screen of defending the honor of its women. This, too, in the face of the fact that only one-third of the 728 victims to mobs have been charged with rape, to say nothing of those of that one-

palliate: downplay, make excuses for.

374 | Ida B. Wells-Barnett

third who were innocent of the charge. A white correspondent of the Baltimore *Sun* declares that the Afro-American who was lynched in Chesterton, Maryland, in May for assault on a white girl was innocent; that the deed was done by a white man who had since disappeared. The girl herself maintained that her assailant was a white man. When that poor Afro-American was murdered, the whites excused their refusal of a trial on the ground that they wished to spare the white girl the **mortification** of having to testify in court.

This cry has had its effect. It closed the heart, stifled the conscience, warped the judgment and hushed the voice of press and pulpit on the subject of lynch law throughout this "land of liberty." Men who stand high in the esteem of the public for Christian character, for moral and physical courage, for devotion to the principles of equal and exact justice to all, and for great **sagacity,** stand as cowards who fear to open their mouths before this great outrage. They do not see that by their **tacit** encouragement, their silent **acquiescence,** the black shadow of lawlessness in the form of lynch law is spreading its wings over the whole country.

Men who, like Governor Tillman, start the ball of lynch law rolling for a certain crime, are powerless to stop it when drunken or criminal white toughs feel like hanging an Afro-American on any pretext.

Even to the better class of Afro-Americans the crime of rape is so revolting they have too often taken the white man's word and given lynch law neither the investigation nor condemnation it deserved.

They forget that a concession of the right to lynch a man for a certain crime, not only concedes the right to lynch any person for any crime, but (so frequently is the cry of rape now raised) it is in a fair way to stamp us a race of rapists and desperadoes. They have gone on hoping and believing that general education and financial strength would solve the difficulty, and are devoting their energies to the accumulation of both.

The mob spirit has grown with the increasing intelligence of the Afro-American. It has left the out-of-the-way places where ignorance prevails, has thrown off the mask and with this new cry stalks in broad daylight in large cities, the cen-

mortification: embarrassment, humiliation.

sagacity: wisdom, intelligence.

tacit: implied but not actually expressed.

acquiescence: acceptance.

ters of civilization, and is encouraged by the "leading citizens" and the press....

[Wells-Barnett then quoted from several newspaper articles that tried to justify lynching as a proper way of dealing with black "criminals."]

[Atlanta newspaper editor and orator] Henry W. Grady in his well-remembered speeches in New England and New York pictured the Afro-American as incapable of self-government. Through him and other leading men the cry of the South to the country has been "Hands off! Leave us to solve our problem." To the Afro-American the South says, "the white man must and will rule." There is little difference between the **Antebellum** South and the New South.

Her white citizens are wedded to any method however revolting, any measure however extreme, for the **subjugation** of the young manhood of the race. They have cheated him out of his ballot, deprived him of civil rights or **redress** therefor in the civil courts, robbed him of the fruits of his labor, and are still murdering, burning and lynching him.

The result is a growing disregard of human life. Lynch law has spread its insid[i]ous influence till men in New York State, Pennsylvania, and on the free Western plains feel they can take the law in their own hands with **impunity,** especially where an Afro-American is concerned. The South is brutalized to a degree not realized by its own inhabitants, and the very foundation of government, law and order, are imperilled.

Public sentiment has had a slight "reaction" though not sufficient to stop the crusade of lawlessness and lynching. The spirit of Christianity of the great M[ethodist] E[piscopal] Church was aroused to the frequent and revolting crimes against a weak people, enough to pass strong condemnatory resolutions at its general conference in Omaha [Nebraska] last May. The spirit of justice of the Grand Old Party [the Republicans] asserted itself sufficiently to secure a denunciation of the wrongs, and a feeble declaration of the belief in human rights in the Republican platform at Minneapolis, [Minnesota] June 7th. Some of the great dailies and weeklies have swung into line declaring that lynch law must go. The president of the United States issued a proclamation that it

antebellum: before the war, in this case the Civil War.

subjugation: defeat, domination.

redress: compensation, a way of righting a wrong done to someone.

impunity: without fear of punishment.

Ida B. Wells-Barnett

be not tolerated in the territories over which he has jurisdiction. Governor Northern and Chief Justice Bleckley of Georgia have proclaimed against it. The citizens of Chattanooga, Tennessee, have set a worthy example in that they not only condemn lynch law, but her public men demanded a trial for [Frank] Weems, [an] accused rapist, and guarded him while the trial was in progress. The trial only lasted ten minutes, and Weems chose to plead guilty and accept twenty-one years sentence, than invite the certain death which awaited him outside that cordon of police if he had told the truth and shown the letters he had from the white woman in the case....

The strong arm of the law must be brought to bear upon lynchers in severe punishment, but this cannot and will not be done unless a healthy public sentiment demands and sustains such action.

The men and women in the South who disapprove of lynching and remain silent on the perpetration of such outrages are *particeps criminis,* accomplices, accessories before and after the fact, equally guilty with the actual lawbreakers who would not persist if they did not know that neither the law nor militia would be employed against them.

In the creation of this healthier public sentiment, the Afro-American can do for himself what no one else can do for him. The world looks on with wonder that we have conceded so much and remain law-abiding under such great outrage and provocation.

To Northern capital and Afro-American labor the South owes its rehabilitation. If labor is withdrawn capital will not remain. The Afro-American is thus the backbone of the South. A thorough knowledge and **judicious** exercise of this power in lynching localities could many times effect a bloodless revolution. The white man's dollar is his god, and to stop this will be to stop outrages in many localities.

The Afro-Americans of Memphis denounced the lynching of three of their best citizens, and urged and waited for the authorities to act in the matter and bring the lynchers to justice. No attempt was made to do so, and the black men left the city by thousands, bringing about great stagnation in every branch of business. Those who remained so injured the

judicious: wise, clever.

business of the streetcar company by staying off the cars, that the superintendent, manager and treasurer called personally on the editor of the *Free Speech,* asked them to urge our people to give them their patronage again. Other businessmen became alarmed over the situation and the *Free Speech* was run away that the colored people might be more easily controlled. A meeting of white citizens in June, three months after the lynching, passed resolutions for the first time, condemning it. But they did not punish the lynchers. Every one of them was known by name, because they had been selected to do the dirty work, by some of the very citizens who passed these resolutions. Memphis is fast losing her black population, who proclaim as they go that there is no protection for the life and property of any Afro-American citizen in Memphis who is not a slave.

The Afro-American citizens of Kentucky, whose intellectual and financial improvement has been phenomenal, have never had a separate car law until now. Delegations and petitions poured into the Legislature against it, yet the bill passed and the Jim Crow Car of Kentucky is a legalized institution. Will the great mass of Negroes continue to patronize the railroad? A special from Covington, Kentucky, says:

> Covington, June 13.—The railroads of the state are beginning to feel very markedly, the effects of the separate coach bill recently passed by the legislature. No class of people in the state have so many and so largely attended excursion as the blacks. All these have been abandoned, and regular travel is reduced to a minimum. A competent authority says the loss to the various roads will reach $1,000,000 this year.

A call to a state conference in Lexington, Kentucky, last June had delegates from every county in the state. Those delegates, the ministers, teachers, heads of secret and other orders, and the head of every family should pass the word around for every member of the race in Kentucky to stay off railroads unless obliged to ride. If they did so, and their advice was followed persistently the convention would not need to petition the legislature to repeal the law or raise money to file a suit. The railroad corporations would be so [a]ffected they would in self-defense lobby to have the separate car law repealed. On the other hand, as long as the railroads can get Afro-American excursions they will always have plenty of money to fight all the suits brought against them. They will be aided in so doing by the same partisan public sentiment which passed the law. White men passed the law, and white judges and juries would pass upon the suits against the law, and render judgment in line with their prejudices and in deference to the greater financial power.

The appeal to the white man's pocket has ever been more effectual than all the appeals ever made to his conscience. Nothing, absolutely nothing, is to be gained by a further sacrifice of manhood and self-respect. By the right exercise of his power as the industrial factor of the South, the Afro-American can demand and secure his rights, the punishment of lynchers, and a fair trial for accused rapists.

Of the many inhuman outrages of this present year, the only case where the proposed lynching did not occur, was where the men armed themselves in Jacksonville, Florida, and Paducah, Kentucky, and prevented it. The only times an Afro-American who was assaulted got away has been when he had a gun and used it in self-defense.

The lesson this teaches and which every Afro-American should ponder well, is that a Winchester rifle should have a place of honor in every black home, and it should be used for that protection which the law refuses to give. When the white man who is always the aggressor knows he runs as great risk of biting the dust every time his Afro-American victim does, he will have greater respect for Afro-American life. The more the Afro-American yields and cringes and begs, the more he has to do so, the more he is insulted, outraged and lynched.

The assertion has been substantiated throughout these pages that the press contains unreliable and doctored reports of lynchings, and one of the most necessary things for the race to do is to get these facts before the public. The people must know before they can act, and there is no educator to compare with the press.

The Afro-American papers are the only ones which will print the truth, and they lack means to employ agents and detectives to get at the facts. The race must rally a mighty host to the support of their journals, and thus enable them to do much in the way of investigation....

[Wells-Barnett emphasized her point by giving several examples of lynchings where additional investigation turned up the real truth behind the alleged crimes.]

The race thus outraged must find out the facts of this awful hurling of men into eternity on supposition, and give them to the indifferent and apathetic country....

No other news goes out to the world save that which stamps us as a race of cut-throats, robbers and lustful wild beasts. So great is Southern hate and prejudice, they legally (?) hung poor little thirteen-year-old Mildrey Brown at Columbia, South Carolina, October 7, on the circumstantial evidence that she poisoned a white infant. If her guilt had been proven unmistakably, had she been white, Mildrey Brown would never have been hung.

The country would have been aroused and South Carolina disgraced forever for such a crime. The Afro-American himself did not know as he should have known, as his journals should be in a position to have him know and act.

Nothing is more definitely settled than [that] he must act for himself. I have shown how he may employ the boycott, emigration and the press, and I feel that by a combination of all these agencies can be effectually stamped out lynch law, that last relic of barbarism and slavery. "The gods help those who help themselves."

99

Sources

Books

Campbell, Karlyn Kohrs, *Man Cannot Speak for Her,* Volume 1: *A Critical Study of Early Feminist Rhetoric,* Volume 2: *Key Texts of the Early Feminists,* Greenwood Press, 1989.

Foner, Philip S., editor, *The Voice of Black America: Major Speeches by Negroes in the United States, 1797–1971,* Simon & Schuster, 1972.

Meltzer, Milton, editor, *The Black Americans: A History in Their Own Words, 1619–1983,* Crowell, 1984.

Wells-Barnett, Ida B., *On Lynchings: Southern Horrors, A Red Record, Mob Rule in New Orleans* (reprints of original pamphlets), Arno, 1969.

Wells-Barnett, Ida B., *Crusader for Justice: The Autobiography of Ida B. Wells,* edited by Alfreda M. Duster, University of Chicago Press, 1970.

George H. White

1852–1918

Politician, lawyer, and businessman

"AFTER ENFORCED DEBAUCHERY WITH MANY KINDRED HORRORS INCIDENT TO SLAVERY, IT COMES WITH ILL GRACE FROM THE PERPETRATORS OF THESE DEEDS TO HOLD UP THE SHORTCOMINGS OF SOME OF OUR RACE TO RIDICULE AND SCORN."

During the two terms (1897–1901) he spent as the only black member of the U.S. House of Representatives, George H. White was a vigorous champion of the rights of African Americans. It was a time of great despair for Southern blacks in particular as they watched the political and social gains they had made after the Civil War slip away. To make matters worse, the mood of the entire nation was becoming increasingly anti-black. White used his position in Congress to do whatever he could to reverse these negative trends. An outstanding public speaker, he often stood up in Congress to talk at length about the notable qualities and positive achievements of African Americans.

Early Life and Career

White was born into slavery in North Carolina and educated in the public schools of that state after the Civil War. He then attended Howard University, from which he received a teaching certificate in 1877. Returning to North

The Freedmen's Bank

In 1865, shortly before the end of the Civil War, the U.S. Congress established the Freedmen's Bank to help newly-freed slaves and their families learn to handle and save money. Almost from the start, however, the Freedmen's Bank was poorly managed. Its officers made risky and even illegal investments, and Congress failed to act on its pledge to appoint someone to monitor the bank's affairs. As a result, after nearly ten years of inefficiency, incompetency, and outright corruption, the Freedmen's Bank failed in 1874, and customers lost the money they had on deposit.

A number of government officials, including President Grover Cleveland in 1886, urged legislators to recognize the country's moral responsibility for the failure. They asked Congress to make sure that the bank's former customers received their money back.

Carolina, White spent several years teaching school and directing an educational facility for other blacks who wanted to be teachers. In 1879, he was admitted to the bar (officially allowed to practice law) in North Carolina and quickly earned a reputation as an excellent lawyer.

White launched his political career the following year (1880) with a victorious run for the state House of Representatives. He remained in office until 1884, when he became one of just two blacks elected to the state senate. Two years later, White easily won election as solicitor (the chief law officer) and prosecuting attorney of the Second Judicial District. He held the position for ten years before making the leap to the U.S. Congress in 1896.

Takes His Place in the U.S. Congress

As the only black member of the House of Representatives, White concentrated on preserving as many rights as possible for African Americans. He took a special interest in legislation involving voting, discrimination, military and private financial relief programs, and the Freedmen's Savings and Trust Company, popularly known as the Freedmen's Bank.

But White's most important act as a legislator took place on February 23, 1900, when he introduced a bill—the first of its kind—that would have made lynching a federal crime. He delivered an impassioned speech to his fellow *representatives in favor of the bill, and they responded with hearty applause. But they hesitated to make lynching a crime subject to the same punishment as treason (the act of overthrowing the government).*

A little less than a year later, White lost his seat to a white Democrat in the 1900 election. On January 29, 1901, the nation's only black representative once again faced fellow members of the House, this time for a farewell address. His memorable parting words are reprinted here from the Congressional Record, *56th Congress, 2nd session, January 29, 1901, pp. 1635-1638.*

I want to enter a plea for the colored man, the colored woman, the colored boy, and the colored girl of this country. I would not thus **digress** from the question at issue and detain the House in a discussion of the interests of this particular people at this time but for the constant and the persistent efforts of certain gentlemen upon this floor to mold and rivet public sentiment against us as a people and to lose no opportunity to hold up the unfortunate few who commit crimes and depredations and lead lives of infamy and shame, as other races do, as fair specimens of representatives of the entire colored race....

In the catalogue of members of Congress in this House perhaps none have been more persistent in their determination to bring the black man into disrepute and, with a labored effort, to show that he was unworthy of the right of citizenship than my colleague from North Carolina, Mr. Kitchin. During the first session of this Congress ... he labored long and hard to show that the white race was at all times and under all circumstances superior to the Negro by inheritance if not otherwise....

He insists and, I believe, has introduced a resolution in this House for the repeal of the Fifteenth Amendment to the Constitution. [The Fifteenth Amendment forbids denying the right to vote to anyone on the basis of race, color, or previous status as a slave.] As an excuse for his peculiar notions

digress: turn away from, change the subject.

about the exercise of the right of **franchise** by citizens of the United States of different nationality, perhaps it would not be amiss to call the attention of this House to a few facts and figures surrounding [Mr. Kitchin's] birth and rearing. To begin with, he was born in one of the counties in my district, Halifax....

I might state as a further general fact that the Democrats of North Carolina got possession of the state and local government since my last election in 1898, and that I bid adieu to these historic walls on the fourth day of next March, and that the brother of Mr. Kitchin will succeed me. Comment is unnecessary. In the town where this young gentleman was born, at the general election last August..., [there was] a registered white vote of 395, most of whom of course were Democrats, and a registered colored vote of 534, virtually if not all of whom were Republicans, and so voted. When the count was announced, however, there were 831 Democrats to 75 Republicans; but in the town of Halifax, same county, the result was much more pronounced.

In that town the registered Republican vote was 345, and the total registered vote of the township was 539, but when the count was announced it stood 990 Democrats to 41 Republicans, or 492 more Democratic votes counted than were registered votes in the township. Comment here is unnecessary, nor do I think it necessary for anyone to wonder at the peculiar notion my colleague has with reference to the manner of voting and the method of counting these votes, nor is it to be a wonder that he is a member of this Congress, having been brought up and educated in such wonderful notions of dealing out fair-handed justice to his fellow man.

It would be unfair, however, for me to leave the **inference** upon the minds of those who hear me that all of the white people of the State of North Carolina hold views with Mr. Kitchin and think as he does. Thank God there are many noble exceptions to the example he sets, that, too, in the Democratic party; men who have never been afraid that one uneducated, poor, depressed Negro could put to flight and chase into degradation two educated, wealthy, thrifty white men. There never has been, nor ever will be, any Negro domination in that state, and no one knows it any better than the

franchise: vote.
inference: suggestion.

Democratic party. It is a convenient howl, however, often resorted to in order to **consummate** a diabolical purpose by scaring the weak and gullible whites into support of measures and men suitable to the **demagogue** and the ambitious office seeker, whose crave for office overshadows and puts to flight all other considerations, fair or unfair.

As I stated on a former occasion, this young statesman has ample time to learn better and more useful knowledge than he has exhibited in many of his speeches upon this floor, and I again plead for him the statute of youth for the wild and spasmodic notions which he has endeavored to rivet upon his colleagues and this country. But I regret that Mr. Kitchin is not alone upon this floor in these peculiar notions advanced. I quote from another young member of Congress, hailing from the State of Alabama [Mr. Underwood]:

> ...When the Fourteenth Amendment was originally adopted it was the intention of the legislative body that enacted it and of the people who ratified it to force the Southern people to give the elective franchise to the Negro. That was the real purpose of the Fourteenth Amendment. It failed in that purpose. The Fifteenth Amendment was adopted for the same purpose. That was successful for the time being. It has proved a **lamentable** mistake, not only to the people of the South, but to the people of the North; not only to the Democratic party, but to the Republican party.
>
> The time has now come when the bitterness of civil strife has passed. The people of the South, with fairness and justice to themselves and fairness to that race that has been forced among them—the Negro race—are attempting to work away from those conditions; not to oppress or to put their foot on the neck of the Negro race, but to protect their homes and their property against misgovernment and at the same time give this inferior race a chance to grow up and acquire their civilization.... I tell you, sirs, there is but one way to solve this problem. You gentlemen of the North, who do not live among them and do not know the conditions, can not solve it.
>
> We of the South are trying, as God is our judge, to solve it fairly to both races. It can not be done in a day or a week.... When we have worked out the problem and put it upon a fair basis, then if we are getting more representation than we are entitled to, five or six or ten years from now come to us with the

consummate: achieve.

demagogue: a leader who appeals to people's prejudices and makes false promises to gain power.

lamentable: sad, regrettable.

proposition fairly to repeal both the Fourteenth and Fifteenth Amendments and substitute in their place a constitutional amendment that will put representation on a basis that we can all agree is fair and equitable. Do not let us drive it along party lines.

It is an undisputed fact that the Negro vote in the State of Alabama, as well as most of the other Southern states, has been effectively suppressed, either one way or the other—in some instances by constitutional amendment and state legislation, in others by cold-blooded **fraud** and **intimidation,** but whatever the method pursued, it is not denied, but frankly admitted in the speeches in this House, that the black vote has been eliminated to a large extent....

Yet the gentleman from Alabama says that the attempt to enforce [the Fourteenth Amendment] is the throwing down of **firebrands,** and notifies the world that this attempt to execute the highest law of the land will be retaliated by the South, and the inference is that the Negro will be even more severely punished than the horrors through which he has already come....

Here's the plain letter of the Constitution, the plain, simple, sworn duty of every member of Congress; yet these gentlemen from the South say, "Yes, we have violated your Constitution of the nation; we regarded it as a local necessity; and now, if you undertake to punish us as the Constitution prescribes, we will see to it that our former deeds of disloyalty to that instrument, our former acts of disfranchisement and opposition to the highest law of the land will be repeated many fold."

Not content with all that has been done to the black man, not because of any deeds that he has done, Mr. Underwood advances the startling information that these people have been thrust upon the whites of the South, forgetting, perhaps, the horrors of the slave trade, the unspeakable horrors of the transit from the shores of Africa by means of the middle passage to the American clime; the enforced bondage of the blacks and their descendants for two and a half centuries in the United States. Now, for the first time perhaps in the history of our lives, the information comes that these poor, helpless, and in the main inoffensive people were thrust upon our Southern brethren....

fraud: cheating, deception, trickery.

intimidation: actions intended to frighten or threaten.

firebrands: something that causes unrest.

I fear I am giving too much time in the consideration of these personal comments of members of Congress, but I trust I will be pardoned for making a passing reference to one more gentleman—Mr. Wilson of South Carolina—who, in the early part of this month, made a speech, some parts of which did great credit to him, showing, as it did, capacity for **collating,** arranging, and advancing thoughts of others and of making a pretty strong argument out of a very poor case.

If he had stopped there, while not agreeing with him, many of us would have been forced to admit that he had done well. But his purpose was incomplete until he dragged in the Reconstruction days and held up to scorn and ridicule the few ignorant, **gullible,** and perhaps purchasable Negroes who served in the state legislature of South Carolina over thirty years ago. Not a word did he say about the **unscrupulous** white men ... who followed in the wake of the Federal Army and settled themselves in the Southern states, and preyed upon the ignorant and unskilled minds of the colored people, looted the states of their wealth, brought into lowest disrepute the ignorant colored people, then hied away to their Northern homes for ease and comfort the balance of their lives, or joined the Democratic party to obtain social recognition, and have greatly aided in depressing and further degrading those whom they had used as tools to accomplish a diabolical purpose. [The "unscrupulous white men" to which White refers were the carpetbaggers, a notorious group of Northerners who migrated to the South during the Reconstruction Era. The carpetbaggers took advantage of the hardships in the South resulting from the war to gain political power as well as vast fortunes. They frequently captured the black vote and thus installed themselves in the South's Republican state governments, where their corrupt activities caused great damage to the restructuring processes of Reconstruction.]

These few ignorant men who chanced at that time to hold office are given as a reason why the black man should not be permitted to participate in the affairs of the government which he is forced to pay taxes to support. He insists that they, the Southern whites, are the black man's best friend, and that they are taking him by the hand and trying to lift him up; that they are educating him. For all that he and all

collating: collecting and comparing.

gullible: trusting.

unscrupulous: corrupt.

George H. White

Southern people have done in this regard, I wish in behalf of the colored people of the South to extend our thanks. We are not ungrateful to friends, but feel that our toil has made our friends able to contribute the **stinty** pittance which we have received at their hands....

If the gentleman to whom I have referred will pardon me, I would like to advance the statement that the musty records of 1868, filed away in the archives of Southern capitols, as to what the Negro was thirty-two years ago, is not a proper standard by which the Negro living on the threshold of the twentieth century should be measured....

[White then recited a wide variety of newer statistics on such topics as education and ownership of property to prove his point that African Americans had come a long way since the end of the Civil War.]

All this was done under the most adverse circumstances. We have done it in the face of lynching, burning at the stake, with the humiliation of "Jim Crow" cars, the disfranchisement of our male citizens, slander and degradation of our women, with the factories closed against us, no Negro permit-

Freed slaves in South awaiting work opportunities

stinty: meager, measly.

ted to be conductor on the railway cars, whether run through the streets of our cities or across the prairies of our great country, no Negro permitted to run as engineer on a locomotive, most of the mines closed against us. Labor unions—carpenters, painters, brick masons, machinists, hackmen and those supplying nearly every conceivable avocation for livelihood—have banded themselves together to better their condition, but, with few exceptions, the black face has been left out. The Negroes are seldom employed in our mercantile stores. At this we do not wonder. Some day we hope to have them employed in our own stores. With all these odds against us, we are forging our way ahead, slowly, perhaps, but surely. You may tie us and then taunt us for a lack of bravery, but one day we will break the bonds. You may use our labor for two and a half centuries and then taunt us for our poverty, but let me remind you we will not always remain poor. You may withhold even the knowledge of how to read God's word and learn the way from earth to glory and then taunt us for our ignorance, but we would remind you that there is plenty of room at the top, and we are climbing.

After enforced debauchery with many kindred horrors incident to slavery, it comes with ill grace from the perpetrators of these deeds to hold up the shortcomings of some of our race to ridicule and scorn....

Mr. Chairman, permit me to digress for a few moments for the purpose of calling the attention of the House to two bills which I regard as important, introduced by me in the early part of the first session of this Congress. The first was to give the United States control and entire jurisdiction over all cases of lynching and death by mob violence. During the last session of this Congress I took occasion to address myself in detail to this particular measure, but with all my efforts the bill still sweetly sleeps in the room of the committee to which it was referred. The necessity of legislation along this line is daily being demonstrated. The arena of the lyncher no longer is confined to Southern climes, but is stretching its **hydra head** over all parts of the Union....

You may dodge this question now; you may defer it to a more seasonable day; ... [but] this evil peculiar to America, yes, to the United States, must be met somehow, some day.

hydra head: an evil that cannot be overcome with a single effort; Hydra was a many-headed serpent in Greek mythology whose heads, when cut off, were each replaced by two more heads.

George H. White

The other bill to which I wish to call attention is one introduced by me to appropriate $1,000,000 to reimburse depositors of the late Freedmen's Savings and Trust Company....

I can not press home to your minds this matter more strongly....

May I hope that the Committee on Banking and Currency who has charge of this measure will yet see its way clear to do tardy justice, long deferred, to this much wronged and unsuspecting people. If individual sections of the country, individual political parties can afford to commit deeds of wrong against us, certainly a great nation like ours will see to it that a people so loyal to its flag as the black man has shown himself in every war from the birth of the Union to this day, will not permit this obligation to go longer uncanceled.

Now, Mr. Chairman, before concluding my remarks I want to submit a brief recipe for the solution of the so-called American Negro problem. He asks no special favors, but simply demands that he be given the same chance for existence, for earning a livelihood, for raising himself in the scales of manhood and womanhood, that are accorded to **kindred** nationalities. Treat him as a man; go into his home and learn of his social conditions; learn of his cares, his troubles and his hopes for the future; gain his confidence; open the doors of industry to him; let the word "Negro," "colored," and "black" be stricken from all the organizations **enumerated** in the federation of labor.

Help him to overcome his weaknesses, punish the crime-committing class by the courts of the land, measure the standard of the race by its best material, cease to mold prejudicial and unjust public sentiment against him, and, my word for it, he will learn to support, hold up the hands of, and join in with that political party, that institution, whether secular or religious, in every community where he lives, which is destined to do the greatest good for the greatest number. Obliterate race hatred, party prejudice, and help us to achieve nobler ends, greater results and become satisfactory citizens to our brother in white.

kindred: similar.
enumerated: counted, listed.

This, Mr. Chairman, is perhaps the Negroes' temporary farewell to the American Congress; but let me say, phoenix-like he will rise up some day and come again. These parting words are in behalf of an outraged, heartbroken, bruised, and bleeding, but God-fearing people, faithful, industrious, loyal people—rising people, full of potential force.

Mr. Chairman, in the trial of Lord Bacon, when the court disturbed the counsel for the defendant, Sir Walter Raleigh raised himself up to his full height and, addressing the court, said, "Sir, I am pleading for the life of a human being."

The only apology that I have to make for the earnestness with which I have spoken is that I am pleading for the life, the liberty, the future happiness, and manhood suffrage for one-eighth of the entire population of the United States.

99

More than twenty-five years would pass before another African American took a seat in the U.S. House of Representatives. After leaving office, White returned to practicing law, first in Washington, D.C., and later in Philadelphia, Pennsylvania. There he opened and operated a bank that helped finance one of his dreams—the establishment of an all-black town. Known as Whitesboro, it was built on the grounds of a former plantation in Cape May County, New Jersey.

Sources

Periodicals

Congressional Record, 56th Congress, 2nd session, January 29, 1901, pp. 1635-1638.

Journal of Negro History, "Four in Black: North Carolina's Black Congressmen, 1874-1901," summer, 1979, pp. 229-243.

Negro History Bulletin, "George Henry White: A Militant Negro Congressman in the Age of Booker T. Washington," March 1966.

Roy Wilkins

1901–1981

Civil rights activist

As head of the National Association for the Advancement of Colored People (NAACP) from 1955 until 1977, Roy Wilkins played a major role in some of the most important battles of the civil rights movement. The tone he set for the NAACP during that period reflected his own quiet, low-key personality. But his conservative leadership style did not appeal to everyone. Some thought that he lacked the proper "fire" to struggle effectively for racial justice. This seemed to be an even bigger shortcoming after the rise of the militant black power movement during the 1960s. Yet by the end of his time in office, most people agreed that Wilkins had done a good job steering the NAACP through an especially difficult time in its history.

Early Life

Wilkins was born in St. Louis, Missouri, but grew up in St. Paul, Minnesota. As a student at the University of Minnesota, he earned a journalism degree and served as the

"NO MATTER HOW ENDLESSLY THEY TRY TO EXPLAIN IT, THE TERM 'BLACK POWER' MEANS ANTI-WHITE POWER."

"ONE COULD THINK BLACK AMERICANS WERE MEN FROM MARS. INSTEAD, WE HAVE BEEN HERE, SIDE BY SIDE WITH THE WHITE FOLKS (SOME OF WHOM JUST GOT HERE), FOR 345 YEARS."

editor of the school newspaper as well as the editor of a local black weekly newspaper. It was also during this time that he first joined the NAACP. He had been drawn to the organization out of concern and horror over several local incidents of racial violence, including the lynching of a black man in the city of Duluth.

After graduating from college, Wilkins took a job with a black weekly newspaper in Missouri, the Kansas City Call. *The rigid segregation and prejudice he experienced there convinced him that African Americans had to take their fight for equality to the courts. So he became even more involved in local NAACP activities. This eventually brought him to the attention of the organization's national leaders. In 1931, they offered Wilkins a job, which he accepted. Thus began his career fighting for an end to discrimination through legal means. It was a cause to which he devoted himself for the next fifty years.*

Rises Through the Ranks to Become NAACP Executive Secretary

From 1931 until he was named executive secretary (head) of the NAACP in 1955, Wilkins served in a variety of administrative positions. One of the most important of these was editor of the NAACP's magazine, Crisis, *a post he held for fifteen years. His investigative work often helped provide the evidence NAACP lawyers needed to bring discrimination complaints to trial. After the cases were settled, Wilkins still kept track of whether people were observing the intent of the law as determined by the court. Later, in his role as executive secretary, Wilkins distinguished himself as a superb manager and one of the civil rights movement's best speakers and writers. Instead of drama and emotion, however, he relied on well-researched facts and a calm, controlled approach to persuade his audiences.*

During the mid- and late 1960s, one of the most serious issues facing mainstream civil rights groups like the NAACP was the growing influence of the black power movement and its leaders. The militancy of Black Panthers **Stokely Carmichael** *(see entry),* **Eldridge Cleaver** *(see entry), and Huey Newton, for example, was especially popular* *with younger African Americans. Many of them had grown impatient with the slow pace of political, social, and economic change. As far as they were concerned, organizations like the NAACP were much too conservative.*

But Wilkins held his ground and absolutely refused to endorse (officially approve) any part of the black power program. This decision angered some people both inside and outside the NAACP. On July 5, 1966, at the group's annual convention (held that year in Los Angeles), Wilkins responded to his critics. Excerpts from his speech are reprinted here from The Rhetoric of the Civil Rights Movement, *edited by Haig A. Bosmajian and Hamida Bosmajian, Random House, 1969.*

" "

All about us are alarums [alarms] and confusions as well as great and challenging developments. Differences of opinion are sharper. For the first time since several organizations began to function where only two had functioned before, there emerges what seems to be a difference in goals.

Heretofore there were some differences in methods and in emphases, but none in ultimate goals. The end was always to be the inclusion of the Negro American, without racial discrimination, as a full-fledged equal in all phases of American citizenship. The targets were whatever barriers, crude or **subtle,** which blocked the attainment of that goal.

There has now emerged, first, a **strident** and threatening challenge to a strategy widely employed by civil rights groups, namely, nonviolence. One organization ... has passed a resolution declaring for defense of themselves by Negro citizens if they are attacked.

This position is not new as far as the NAACP is concerned. Historically our association has defended in courts those persons who have defended themselves and their homes with firearms. **Extradition** cases are not as frequent or as fashionable as they once were, but in past years we have fought the extradition of men who had used firearms to defend themselves when attacked....

subtle: hidden, obscured.

strident: harsh, loud.

extradition: the process of turning over a suspected criminal from one state to another so that he or she can stand trial in the state where the crime was supposedly committed.

The NAACP has subscribed to nonviolence as a humane as well as a practical necessity in the realities of the American scene, but we have never required this as a deep personal commitment of our members. We never signed a pact either on paper or in our hearts to turn the other cheek forever and ever when we were assaulted.

But neither have we **couched** a policy of manly resistance in such a way that our members and supporters felt **compelled** to maintain themselves in an armed state, ready to retaliate instantly and in kind whenever attacked. We venture the observation that such a publicized posture could serve to stir counter-planning, counter-action and possible conflict. If carried out literally as instant retaliation, in cases adjudged by **aggrieved** persons to have been grossly unjust, this policy could produce—in extreme situations—lynchings, or, in better-sounding **phraseology,** private, **vigilante** vengeance.

Moreover, in attempting to substitute for **derelict** law enforcement machinery, the policy **entails** the risk of a broader, more **indiscriminate** crackdown by law officers, under the ready-made excuse of restoring law and order.

It seems reasonable to assume that proclaimed protective violence is as likely to encourage counter-violence as it is to discourage violent persecution.

But the more serious division in the civil rights movement is the one posed by a word formulation that implies clearly a difference in goals.

No matter how endlessly they try to explain it, the term "black power" means anti-white power. In a racially **pluralistic** society, the concept, the formation and the exercise of an ethnically-tagged power, means opposition to other ethnic powers, just as the term "white supremacy" means subjection of all nonwhite people. In the black-white relationship, it has to mean that every other ethnic power is the rival and the **antagonist** of "black power." It has to mean "going-it-alone." It has to mean separatism.

Now, separatism, whether on the **rarefied** debate level of "black power" or on the wishful level of a **secessionist** Freedom City in Watts, offers a disadvantaged minority little except the chance to shrivel and die.

couched: expressed.

compelled: forced.

aggrieved: injured, wronged.

phraseology: choice of words.

vigilante: a member of a volunteer group that quickly hunts down and punishes suspected criminals without a trial.

derelict: careless, neglectful.

entails: involves.

indiscriminate: random, disorganized.

pluralistic: diverse, displaying many different qualities.

antagonist: enemy.

rarefied: abstract, theoretical.

secessionist: withdrawn or broken away from.

Roy Wilkins

The only possible dividend of "black power" is embodied in its offer to millions of frustrated and deprived and persecuted black people of a **solace,** a tremendous psychological lift, quite apart from its political and economic implications.

Ideologically it dictates "up with black and down with white"....

It is a reverse Mississippi, a reverse Hitler, a reverse Ku Klux Klan.

If these were evil in our judgment, what virtue can be claimed for black over white? If, as some **proponents** claim, this concept instills pride of race, cannot this pride be taught without preaching hatred or supremacy based upon race?

Though it be **clarified** and clarified again, "black power" in the quick, uncritical and highly emotional adoption it has received from some segments of a **beleaguered** people can mean in the end only black death....

We of the NAACP will have none of this. We have fought it too long. It is the ranging of race against race on the **irrelevant** basis of skin color. It is the father of hatred and the mother of violence.

It is the wicked **fanaticism** which has swelled our tears, broken our bodies, squeezed our hearts and taken the blood of our black and white loved ones. It shall not now poison our forward march.

We seek, therefore, as we have sought these many years, the inclusion of Negro Americans in the nation's life, not their exclusion. This is our land, as much so as it is any American's—every square foot of every city and town and village. The task of winning our share is not the easy one of **disengagement** and flight, but the hard one of work, of short as well as long jumps, of disappointments, and of sweet successes.

In our Fight for Freedom we choose:

1. The power and the majesty of the ballot, the participation of free men in their government, both as voters and as honorable and competent elected and appointed public servants....

solace: comfort, relief.

proponents: promoters, supporters.

clarified: explained.

beleaguered: troubled, harassed.

irrelevant: not applicable, having no relation to the matter at hand.

fanaticism: intense and often excessive and uncritical devotion to someone or something.

disengagement: withdrawal.

2. We choose employment for our people—jobs not hidden by racial labels or **euphemisms,** not limited by racial restrictions in access and promotion, whether by employers or organized labor.....

3. We choose to combat the color line in housing. In one breath our opinion-makers **decry** the existence of the poverty and filth and crime and degradation of the slums, but in the next they decry low-cost housing and fair housing laws.... One could think black Americans were men from Mars. Instead, we have been here, side by side with the white folks (some of whom just got here), for 345 years.

   They tell us to work hard and save our money, to go to school and prepare ourselves, to be "responsible," to rear and educate our children in a wholesome and directed family atmosphere, to achieve, to "get up in the world."

   After we do all this, they look us in the eye and bar us from renting or buying a home that matches our achievements and one in keeping with our aspirations for further advancement....

4. Most of all, we choose to secure unsegregated, high quality public education for ourselves and our children....

   The longer our children attend racially segregated schools, the farther they fall behind white children....

   Before we can get jobs to earn increased income to buy and rent better homes, before we can contribute to the enrichment of our nation, we must have free access to quality education.

   The man who shoots and burns and drowns us is surely our enemy, but so is he who cripples our children for life with inferior public education.

5. We also choose to wrestle with the complex problems of urban life, all of which include an attitude toward and a treatment of millions of Negro citizens....

euphemisms: inoffensive substitutions for a word or expression that might otherwise be offensive.

decry: criticize, condemn.

The police everywhere can make or break urban racial tensions by their conduct toward minority group citizens.

Last summer you had here an upheaval that shook the world. [Wilkins is referring here to the violent racial disturbances in the Watts section of Los Angeles in August 1965.] To many of us who looked from afar, it appeared to be a wild, senseless rampage of hate and destruction. But that was far from the whole truth.

There was powder in Watts, piled up and packed down through the years: wide-scale unemployment, both adult and teenage, slum housing, crowded schools, nonexistent health facilities, inadequate transportation and—the [Los Angeles] police attitude. Everyone was suspect and everyone was subject to harassment in one form or another. The community **smoldered** under the peculiar brand that police place upon a whole section with their constant sirens, their **contemptuous** searches, their rough talk, their ready guns and their general "Godalmightiness."

The lesson they and city officials have learned from last year is to seek not correction and improvement, but still more **repression.....**

The McCone Report on the 1965 riot called for "costly and extreme" remedies for Watts, undertaken with a "revolutionary attitude." The answer of the City of Los Angeles was to vote down a hospital bond issue. The answer of Mayor Yorty and of his man, [police] Chief Parker, is a trampling-tough riot-control bill which, if enacted, would loose the police, almost without restraint, upon a populace sick to death—literally—of race control. To blot out any remaining fitful light, one of the **gubernatorial** candidates ... is the darling of those ultra-conservatives who believe in iron control of what they call "violence in the streets"—their code name for Negroes.

If this is the best that a great city can bring to a hard urban problem, one largely of its own making, then God pity both the whites and the Negroes!

smoldered: quietly burned with hidden anger and hate.

contemptuous: showing scorn.

repression: the act of restraining someone or something by force.

gubernatorial: of or relating to the political office of governor.

We have no **panacea** for all these problems. We do not proclaim that what we declare here this week is going to change the course of the whole civil rights movement. We do not know all the answers to the George Wallace problem in Alabama, the James Eastland problem in Mississippi, or to the Boston, Massachusetts, school committee and its Louise Day Hicks problem. We certainly don't know the answers to foreign policy and to tax and interest rate puzzlers.

But in this unsettled time when shifts are the order of the day and when change is in the air, we can sail our NAACP ship "steady as she goes," with more drive to the turbines, more skill at the wheel, but no fancy capers for the sake of capers.

We can follow down into each community the really advanced blueprint of the White House Conference "To Fulfill These Rights," which covered four principal areas: economic security and welfare, education, housing, and the administration of justice.

We can expand and point up the community services of our NAACP branches, each of which is, in reality, a citizenship clinic. Just as medical clinics need specialists to cure physical ills, so our branch clinics should recruit volunteer specialists to diagnose and minister to social ills.

We must involve people in the communities in the solution of our problem—not limiting ourselves to our church or lodge or club group.

We must keep the pressure on our local and state education systems through the employment of every legitimate technique: protests, surveys, discussions, demonstrations, picketing and negotiation. Nothing should be overlooked in fighting for better education. Be persistent and ornery; this will be good for the lethargic educational establishment and will aid the whole cause of public education....

In a world where the mayor of Los Angeles is yelling "riot control," where Rhodesia says "never!" to black representation while in America SNCC [Student Nonviolent Coordinating Committee] raises the chant of black power, where the federal government at long last is committed, but both the far right and the far left offer vocal and vicious objection,

panacea: remedy, cure-all.

someone has to drive the long haul toward the group goal of Negro Americans and the larger ideal of our young nation.

Our objective is basically as it was laid down in 1909 by the interracial founders of our NAACP. Back [then they] expressed the strong feeling that the first NAACP conference "will utter no uncertain sound on any point affecting the vital subject. No part of it is too delicate for plain speech. The republican experiment is at stake, every tolerated wrong to the Negro reacting with double force upon white citizens guilty of faithlessness to their brothers."

As it was then, so it is today. The republican experiment is at stake in 1966. More than that, the dream of a brotherhood in equality and justice is imperiled.

Our fraternity tonight, as it was then, is the fraternity of man, not the white, or brown, or yellow, or black man, but man.

99

Sources

Books

Bosmajian, Haig A., and Hamida Bosmajian, editors, *The Rhetoric of the Civil Rights Movement,* Random House, 1969.

Boulware, Marcus H., *The Oratory of Negro Leaders: 1900-1968,* Negro Universities Press, 1969.

Foner, Philip S., editor, *The Voice of Black America: Major Speeches by Negroes in the United States, 1797-1971,* Simon & Schuster, 1972.

Smith, Arthur L., and Stephen Robb, editors, *The Voice of Black Rhetoric: Selections,* Allyn & Bacon, 1971.

Wilkins, Roy, with Tom Mathews, *Standing Fast: The Autobiography of Roy Wilkins,* Viking, 1982.

Williams, Jamye Coleman, and McDonald Williams, editors, *The Negro Speaks: The Rhetoric of Contemporary Black Leaders,* Noble and Noble, 1970.

Whitney M. Young, Jr.

1921–1971

Social worker and civil rights leader

One of the giants of the civil rights movement of the 1960s was Whitney M. Young, Jr., who served for ten tumultuous years as executive director of the National Urban League (NUL). The NUL was a civil rights organization dedicated to helping blacks who had moved from rural areas to the nation's cities adjust to their new lives. Within just a few years after taking over the top spot at the NUL in 1961, Young had changed its image and given it a burst of much-needed energy. More significantly, he had personally emerged to become one of his generation's most forceful and outspoken advocates of changes that promised to reverse several hundred years of neglect.

Early Life

A native of Kentucky, Young was one of three children. His father was the director of a boarding high school for blacks, and his mother was a teacher. After graduating from the school his father headed, Young attended Ken-

tucky State College and earned his bachelor's degree in studies aimed at preparing him to become a doctor. He then spent about a year as a high school teacher and assistant principal.

Around 1942, during World War II, Young entered the military and was sent to study engineering at the Massachusetts Institute of Technology (MIT). Eventually, he headed overseas with an anti-aircraft artillery group. His experiences—both good and bad—as a black army private under the command of a white Southern captain made him reconsider his choice of a career in medicine. Upon returning to the United States, Young enrolled in the social work program at the University of Minnesota. He received his master's degree in 1947.

From 1947 until 1950, Young worked in St. Paul, Minnesota, as director of industrial relations and vocational guidance for the local branch of the National Urban League. He also lectured at the nearby College of St. Catherine. Young then moved on to Omaha, Nebraska, to serve as head of that city's NUL chapter. During this period, he taught in the School of Social Work at both the University of Nebraska and Creighton University. As the civil rights movement began gaining strength in the South, however, Young wanted very much to be a part of it. Thus, in 1954 he headed to Georgia's Atlanta University to become dean of its School of Social Work.

Named Head of the National Urban League

In 1961, Young was named the new head of the National Urban League, which was then at a critical point in its existence. Founded in New York City in 1910, it had operated basically as a social-work agency that focused on the economic problems of urban blacks in the North, especially those who had moved from rural areas of the South. The conservative blacks who ran the NUL had tried to obtain job training and placement for African American industrial workers by joining together with white businessmen. In this way, they hoped to improve the standard of living for urban blacks. But as the struggle for civil rights began to heat up during the early 1960s, the NUL approach seemed totally out of step with the times.

Under Young's leadership, the organization was reborn. Its new image reflected his own personal energy as well as his impatience with the slow pace of improvement—especially economic improvement—in the status of African Americans. Young used the NUL's long-established ties with white corporate and political leaders to bring about change. But because he was so willing to work with whites, he often had to put up with the insults of more militant blacks who called him an *"Uncle Tom."*

The outspoken and **articulate** Young turned out to be an ideal choice to promote the NUL's new mission. He contributed numerous articles and columns to magazines and newspapers and spoke regularly to audiences throughout the United States about his ideas for fighting unemployment, poverty, and hopelessness in the black community.

In 1963, for example, Young proposed what he called his "domestic Marshall Plan." (This was a reference to the massive U.S. rebuilding program after World War II that provided huge amounts of aid to European countries to help them recover from the effects of wartime destruction.) As part of this plan, Young suggested that African Americans deserved special treatment to make up for years of slavery and segregation. This controversial statement pushed him into the national spotlight for the first—but certainly not the last—time.

On July 19, 1970, Young delivered an address to the annual convention of the National Urban League, held that year in New York City. In his speech, he discussed the victories and the failures of the 1960s, a decade of great upheaval and change. And in blunt yet moving terms, he looked ahead to the 1970s and the new challenges facing African Americans. An excerpt from his remarks follows. It is reprinted from the September 15, 1970, issue of Vital Speeches.

"Uncle Tom": a black who is overeager to win the approval of whites. (Uncle Tom was a faithful slave in Harriet Beecher Stowe's 1851 novel, *Uncle Tom's Cabin.*)

articulate: capable of expressing oneself well.

❝

    There comes a time in the life of every great nation when it finds itself at the crossroads—on one side, the path of division, decline, and **oblivion;** on the other, the path of progress, purpose, and decency. There is every indication that this nation ... is at that crossroads.

oblivion: being forgotten or unknown.

Whitney M. Young, Jr.

At every hand we see chaos instead of concern, drift instead of decision, and hate instead of hope. It may well be that we are witnessing the exhaustion of the American spirit; the full-scale retreat by a people **nurturing** false dreams of superiority; a retreat from the responsibilities and decency that characterize true greatness....

The signs ... are unmistakable that this unhappy land, this bitterly **polarized** society, seems incapable of living up to the ideals and dreams that it **purportedly** held for so long....

Repression is **rampant.** Americans—for the first time in decades—now have their own "show" trials, political prisoners, and midnight police raids that kill people in their beds, people whose crime was **dissent** from a society that persecuted them.

And fanning the flames of repression have been the mindless **pseudo-revolutionists** of the left whose idea of changing society is to plant bombs where they might kill the innocent—and the mindless pseudo-conservatives of the right whose idea of standing up for the democracy they are sworn to protect is to destroy it through division and hate....

Beset by the twin evils of repression and **recession,** black people today are fearful that the limited gains of the sixties are in danger. We have seen that in spite of legal and legislative victories, racism is still alive in new and different forms....

It has become more clear than ever, that the black man's fight for respect and for manhood is also a fight to right the wrongs of a bloated, sick society, and to bring it back to its senses....

The Urban League, at this stage of its history, has the responsibility to continue in its efforts to pull together America's minority communities in order to **mobilize** its enormous **reservoir** of talent and skills to win political, economic, and social victories....

For, in this our sixtieth year, the Urban League has evolved far from the limited functions envisioned by its founders. The social services we once provided newcomers to the cities of the North have had to be supplemented and replaced by a much more comprehensive organization of the black com-

nurturing: furthering the development of.

polarized: divided into two opposing sides.

purportedly: supposedly.

repression: the act of putting down something or someone by force.

rampant: widespread.

dissent: protest, disagreement.

pseudo-revolutionists: false or phony revolutionaries.

recession: an economic slowdown.

mobilize: bring together in an orderly and effective way.

reservoir: supply.

Whitney M. Young, Jr.

munity. Two years ago ... the Urban League moved into the ghetto—physically and spiritually—and is serving as an **enabling vehicle** for a black community determined to win unity, dignity, and power....

For we believe that "Power to the People" is but an empty phrase unless the people can be provided with the mechanism, technical assistance, and opportunities to make that power work for them in their own communities, on their own terms, under their own leadership. And a clenched fist is useless, if, when forced open, it is found to be empty of the resources of money, **intellect,** and the will to do the job....

The Urban League movement continues to be flexible, **relevant,** and vital. We have successfully shifted gears from treating the results of racism and poverty to mounting a full-scale attack on the *causes* of racism and poverty. The Urban League has taken on a commitment to change the institutions and the society that **perpetuates** injustice....

But we cannot be **complacent** about our successes, accomplished with limited resources. They represent a challenge for still greater efforts in the future; a base from which we must build the **coalitions** and unity without which racism will remain supreme, and poverty will possess the souls of the real forgotten Americans—the blacks, the browns, and the reds of the rural and urban ghettos.

This new decade could bring promise of a new era in the relations between the races. Just as the nation as a whole is at a crossroads, so, too, black people face a new turning point, a decisive strategic moment that may put us on a new path to freedom. Just as there is some doubt whether the nation will choose the right path to greatness there must be doubts, especially in the light of the historic racism of America, that the seventies will bring true equality for black people. But while we may question the future, it becomes our duty to mobilize and steel ourselves for a new phase of struggle....

It is obvious that where blacks are concerned, the administration [of President Richard Nixon] faces a **credibility gap** of enormous proportions. But it persists in claiming that the record does not justify this suspicion; that progress is being made, and that it does not intend to abandon blacks to the evil **expedient** of a Southern strategy that tries to out-Wal-

enabling vehicle: a provider of the resources needed to make things happen.

intellect: the capacity to think rationally and intelligently.

relevant: having a direct bearing on the matter at hand.

perpetuates: causes to continue.

complacent: contented with, self-satisfied.

coalitions: alliances of different people or groups who come together to take action.

credibility gap: lack of trust and believability.

expedient: something that can be carried out quickly and efficiently.

lace Wallace. [Young is referring here to former Alabama Governor George Wallace, who was for many years an outspoken segregationist.]

The record is sometimes muddied. As critical as I have been of [Nixon] administration actions, I do admit that there are some signs that elements of this administration are moving forward to bring about change.... It would be a mistake for us to fail to recognize that within every administration there are contending forces. To cease to fight for our victories and to fail to negotiate with those in power is to leave the field to the political **Neanderthals** that so far seem to have dominated decision-making in the past few years.

Early in his administration, the president asked black Americans to judge him by his deeds and not his words. We have done that—and we have been greatly disappointed.... Black people have—with justification—always judged white America with suspicion and disappointment. Promises have rarely led to performance, and words as well as well-meaning deeds have often been traps to further ensnare us.

We have been forced by this administration to react with defensive measures, if not actual confrontation, and perhaps now a new strategy would be more fitting. For these tactics were based on protest born of powerlessness. I believe that we have demonstrated that we do have some power now—power to make America sit and listen, and to negotiate with us as equal partners. America can no longer afford to ignore its awakened black masses. And no administration—unless it is willing to preside over the destruction of American democracy, can afford to refuse the just demands of its neglected minorities.

While we would hope that the nation's leadership would exercise the kind of determined, crusading sense of mission that is the **hallmark** of great leadership, it is a fact of life that there is developing a national stand-off between those of us who are fighting for justice and those who want to maintain the **status quo.**

This is an **impasse** that leads nowhere, unless it be to further polarization, further division, further bitterness. White society has shown that it lacks the courage and the imagina-

Neanderthals: people whose ideas or behavior are primitive and simple-minded.

hallmark: sign.

status quo: the existing state of affairs.

impasse: stand-off, deadlock.

Whitney M. Young, Jr.

tion to break this impasse by moving constructively. It is up to the black community to show the way.

Our cause is just. But white America still possesses the power. We must forge the union of justice with power....

I propose that the just and the powerful deal with each other as equals in a *strategy of negotiation.*

White society has the **trappings** of power—its police, its army, its law. But blacks have demonstrated effectively that unless our just demands are dealt with, these trappings of power only make a society muscle-bound; only drive it into displays of raw, naked power, displays that solve nothing and tear apart everything.

The two Americas—black and white—need each other. Let us break the rigid confines of charges and countercharges, protest and neglect. Let us negotiate our way out of the impasse that threatens to split the country apart.

By all means, we must continue to confront injustice. A strategy of negotiation does not imply weakness; on the contrary, it implies strength—the strength a unified black community can demonstrate....

Such a strategy demands from white America that it face up to the realities of a situation in which black young men are sent thousands of miles from home [to Vietnam] to fight and die for a cause labeled democracy, while democracy is denied them in the swollen ghettos of New York and in the sullen farmlands of Mississippi.

It demands from white America that it **implement** a massive domestic Marshall Plan that will rescue all Americans from poverty and disease.

And above all, it demands from white America that it demonstrate the will, the honesty, and the sincerity to face its black brothers on equal terms, as peers in a joint effort to rid the nation of the cancer of racism.

A strategy of negotiation demands from black America the power to negotiate from a position of strength. I believe we have demonstrated that power.... We have made the most of the limited opportunities available to the point where we have the pride, the strength, and the accomplishments

trappings: outward signs or symbols.
implement: carry out.

which should **compel** white leadership to sit down with us as equals.

A strategy of negotiation demands of black leadership a sense of unity and purpose.... It will demand of us a discipline and a willingness to rise above differences of **doctrine** and personality for the greater good of all black people. We must, more than ever, impose upon ourselves and our organizations a community of spirit and a fraternal bond that will enable us to better negotiate from a base of strength and unity....

It will not be easy to achieve such unity, because there are those whose experiences have led them to **despair** of white America ever acting in a decent way. But I have confidence that black people will muster the courage and the strength to make one last effort, based on our common sufferings, to stand united against the system that **oppresses** us.

And for America, this may be the last opportunity she has to deal with black Americans and to negotiate with leaders responsible to their people, before the terrifying prospect of internal strife, armed suppression and needless destruction descend fully upon us all.

Black unity is essential for black progress. This is no time for divisions.... Only by unified action can we break the bonds that chain us. Only by unified action can we force America to become moral. Only by unified action can we forge the alliances across racial lines that promise progress.

And only through unity can we cut through the undergrowth of myth and misunderstanding and unite with other minorities to forge a new coalition for a better tomorrow.

I know that blacks have often been suspicious of such alliances. We have become contemptuous of an America that has "discovered" its problems so recently, although we have struggled with them for so long. We sense that other causes have higher priority than our own....

But we must not let ourselves become imprisoned by concepts of race that ignore the other causes of our misery.....

The economic and power dimensions of the problems facing us can be met through alliances with others in this twisted society who are hurting, too.

compel: force.

doctrine: belief.

despair: lose all hope.

oppresses: crushes or persecutes through the abuse of power or authority.

Whitney M. Young, Jr.

The problems of poverty are not black alone. There is hunger in the tenements and shacks of whites and browns and reds as well. There is misery in Appalachian ghost towns, in the barrios of the West, in migrant labor camps, and in Indian reservations. And there is misery here in New York's Harlem, South Bronx, and Bedford Stuyvesant.

America has grown fat and heavy with the sweat and labor of all minorities, now she must grow proud and strong through an alliance based on our realism and sense of purpose. There is at hand the raw material for building the strong alliance for social justice that is essential if America is to be saved—and we must save her if we are not *all* to go down the drain. While it is an historic fact that we came here on different ships, it is **imperative** that we realize that we're in the same boat now....

I believe that the many **disparate** and contending forces in our society today, the diverse people and groups trying to

Young speaking out: "Let us negotiate our way out of the impasse that threatens to split the country apart."

imperative: absolutely necessary.

disparate: different.

change some small corner of American life, can be brought to see how racism and mindless **materialism** work hand-in-hand to turn the American dream into a nightmare.

And I believe that—whether because they pursue their own self-interest or because they move their idealism to a higher, more realistic plane—a new coalition can be forged that will once more return America to a sense of purpose and a will to justice....

The proud black spirit of today seeks justice and decency. It seeks to move beyond racism to a new era of progress and reconciliation. It seeks power not for its own sake, but in order to use it wisely and to prevent its misuse by racism. It seeks peace with honor, justice with respect. It seeks a newer world, and a better tomorrow....

99

This speech marked the last time Young spoke at the annual convention of the National Urban League. Eight months later, on March 11, 1971, he suffered a heart attack and drowned while swimming off the coast of Nigeria. He had been part of a group of black and white Americans who were visiting the city of Lagos for a special conference aimed at creating closer ties between blacks in Africa and the United States.

Sources

Books

Baraka, Imamu Amiri (LeRoi Jones), editor, *African Congress: A Documentary of the First Modern Pan-African Congress,* Morrow, 1972.

Boulware, Marcus H., *The Oratory of Negro Leaders: 1900–1968,* Negro Universities Press, 1969.

Broderick, Francis L., and August Meier, editors, *Negro Protest Thought in the Twentieth Century,* Bobbs-Merrill, 1965.

Foner, Philip S., editor, *The Voice of Black America: Major Speeches by Negroes in the United States, 1797–1971,* Simon & Schuster, 1972.

materialism: excessive interest in things than can be bought and possessed rather than in things of an intellectual or spiritual nature.

Whitney M. Young, Jr.

Hale, Frank W., Jr., *The Cry for Freedom: An Anthology of the Best That Has Been Said and Written on Civil Rights since 1954,* A. S. Barnes, 1969.

Thonssen, Lester, editor, *Representative American Speeches: 1966–1967,* Wilson, 1967.

Weiss, Nancy J., *Whitney M. Young, Jr., and the Struggle for Civil Rights,* Princeton University Press, 1989.

Williams, Jamye Coleman, and McDonald Williams, *The Negro Speaks: The Rhetoric of Contemporary Black Leaders,* Noble & Noble, 1970.

Young, Whitney M., Jr., *To Be Equal,* McGraw-Hill, 1964.

Young, Whitney M., Jr., *Beyond Racism: Building an Open Society,* McGraw-Hill, 1969.

Periodicals

Ebony, "America Mourns Whitney M. Young, Jr.," May 1971.

Newsweek, "Whitney Young: He Was Doer," March 22, 1971, p. 29.

New York Times, March 12, 1971; March 13, 1971.

New York Times Magazine, "Whitney Young: Black Leader or 'Oreo Cookie'?" September 20, 1970.

Time, "Kind of Bridge," March 22, 1971, p. 20.

Vital Speeches, "The Intermingled Revolutions," September 1, 1964, pp. 692-694; "The Positive Side of the Racial Story," July 1, 1965, pp. 572-576; "A New Thrust Toward Economic Security," October 1, 1969, pp. 759-763; "A Strategy for the Seventies," September 15, 1970, pp. 732-736.

Index

Bolds indicate featured speakers and volume numbers; illustrations are marked (ill.).